CU01494926

....

Here is a year's worth of ready-made NLP pract

It's for the millions of people all over the world who love NLP and who want to deepen their skills and have fun together practising and experimenting with the core practitioner curriculum.

The book also offers a stimulating and rewarding introduction to the contemporary field of NLP and shows you how to apply NLP tools and skills effectively to both your personal and professional issues.

Compiled and introduced by *Judith Lowe,* with forewords by NLP co-developers *Robert Dilts* and *Judith DeLozier,* each chapter offers practical knowledge and step-by-step instructions to make the topics easy to follow and rewarding to understand. All the contributors are experts in their own application areas and experienced in advanced NLP. They share their stories, their models and some of their tips for success, making each chapter a uniquely fascinating exploration of a particular topic.

You can learn how to be more resilient, negotiate well, coach in a limited time frame, enhance your leadership skills, study effectively, network, communicate expertly, nurture your intimate relationships, enrich your creativity... and much, much more.

All of this is supported by an introductory NLP manual and a checklist for running a successful practice group.

The PPD Learning NLP Practice Group Book is packed with ideas and practical suggestions for NLP enthusiasts – there's something for everyone in these pages!

....

1

"Well, done, Judith - What a fantastic collaborative book, gathering ideas and exercises for Practice Group facilitators to delve into and enjoy...there must be at least a year's worth of material for Practice Group meetings contained in this gem of a book.

We are great advocates of Practice Groups...after all, becoming an NLP Practitioner is a little like passing one's driving test – the real practice starts once the test has been passed! So we are delighted to support any venture which provides additional resources for Practice Groups around the UK...and beyond."

Karen Moxom
Managing Director ANLP

The NLP Practice Group Book is for organisers of NLP Practice Groups as well as coaches/therapists, managers, educators and individuals who benefit from self-directed learning. There is wealth of knowledge to be had from each chapter written by a specialist in the field. These demonstrate the diverse richness of NLP applied to topics that affect us all. And the numerous activities provided will support you to go beyond understanding to embodying the experience. Having run NLP Practice groups for many years, we know the difference this book can make to those who seek a path to mastery. It is a genuine contribution to an important area of NLP that is seldom put in the spotlight.

Penny Tompkins and James Lawley
Authors, Metaphors in Mind: Transformation Through Symbolic Modeling

"This book is such a brilliant idea. It introduces, highlights and captures the ethos, essence and contribution of a successful NLP Practice Group to participants. It is an inspirational, practical and rich resource of 'How to run a session in a nutshell' with subjects, learning objectives and exercise guidance clearly laid out and explained. Guest speakers generously share their personal expertise, around a breadth of subjects and contexts, that can be introduced and immediately utilised to enhance the learning and application of NLP in different contexts."

Henrietta Laitt
Richmond NLP Group

The NLP Practice Group Book from Judith Lowe and PPD Learning is a wonderful and inspirational contribution to all the big and small practice groups out there helping to keep the spirit of curiosity and learning alive. All of the articles are beautifully framed and explained, the exercises produce measurable and meaningful outputs, and work with all levels of skills and experience. In short they fit perfectly into the typical practice group structure of a few hours dedicated to NLP every so many weeks, come one come all. Viewed as a whole they demonstrate the depth and breadth we can reach with simple NLP ideas and tools and will motivate and inspire groups everywhere to create, to model, to share - to practise.

Sean Owen-Moylan
Co-creator Cardiff NLP Practice Group

I really enjoyed reading this book of authentic richness. It is engaging, easy to read and unpretentious. None of these writers pretend to be gurus, they are just ordinary people dedicated to applying NLP to cope with the complexities of living in the 21st Century. They have shared their own learnings and experiences with other practitioners and doubtless have already added value to the lives of many. Now they are taking the opportunity to share further, through a different medium, whilst adding value to, and expanding the field of NLP.

They gently take on a challenge, which anyone involved in facilitating NLP faces whether they realise it or not, and that is how to develop the field. The originators are a small and ageing group; new and creative work generated collaboratively, by modelling those early methods and sharing applications is urgently required and here we have a sound contribution from motivated and genuine people, who have honed their craft as a team whilst keeping their individuality through diverse offerings.

I recommend this book to anyone interested in 'being' human – whether from business, health, education or sport we can all learn from these reflections.

Dr Sally Vanson
Executive Coach and Director of NLP based post graduate programmes

I am enjoying savouring the chapters. I really relish this display of 'feminine' NLP at work and it is a pleasure to immerse myself with people who share my values of relationship. A lovely collection and it does speak so well of your work and efforts of the last mumble mumble number of years. You should feel well proud.

Fran Burgess
Author of The Bumper Bundle Book of Modelling and The NLP Cookbook

What I love about this book is the way that Judith and the contributors are able to be both transformational and highly rigorous at the same time. To become an NLP Maestro, just like becoming a concert pianist, requires a dedicated approach - I am sure you'll find the way within these pages!

Robbie Steinhouse
The NLP School and Author of How to Coach with NLP

This book contains a small number of select and well described examples of excellence in human attributes. All of these examples are the result of rigorous modelling, followed by a commitment to making them accessible to others.

I am privileged to have seen Judith Lowe exquisitely support other people's development of many such skills.

No doubt there are many other good books out there. This is amongst the best of them.

Neil Harris
NLP Trainer and Coach

This book contains real life ways to approach solving a variety of common 'problems' we see in our day to day lives. It has been written by an outstanding collection of practitioners from business and coaching backgrounds. Forget the jargon this is a great guide for anyone interested in new perspectives and methods of change. Buy it and try them out for yourself !

Sean Finnan
Non-executive and MD SF&A Coaching, MSc in NLP

The PPD Learning

NLP Practice Group Book

The special guest sessions

Judith Lowe

Forewords by Robert Dilts & Judith DeLozier

Published by Maxfield Press

Foreword by Robert Dilts

I have long maintained that one of the distinguishing features of Neuro Linguistic Programming (NLP), and one of the reasons that its use has spread throughout the world, is that it has developed and evolved less through theories and laboratory research than it has through the heuristic approach of applied practice. The PPD Learning NLP Practice Group Book is an excellent demonstration of that assertion.

As modern dance pioneer Martha Graham pointed out, "We learn by practice. Whether it means to learn to dance by practising dancing or to learn to live by practising living, the principles are the same . . . Practice is a means of inviting the perfection desired." Since its founding more than 40 years ago, NLP has emphasized the importance of interactive practice as the foundation for personal growth and development.

As a member of the early "META groups" run by Richard Bandler and John Grinder in the 1970s, I witnessed and experienced the profound and generative impact of practice as a way to both embody and creatively explore the transformational principles and skills that were to become NLP. In fact, one of my favourite sayings is the New Guinea proverb which states, "Knowledge is only a rumour until it is in the muscle." Knowledge gets "into the muscle" through practice.

The PPD Learning NLP Practice Group Book is a collection of diverse exercises illustrating the impressive and ever expanding range of applications of NLP. These exercises explore how NLP can be pragmatically applied to such varied areas as coaching, creativity, leadership, resilience, negotiation, study skills, strengthening relationships, communication and even horse training. An exceptional collaborative effort, the book is also an example of how collective intelligence is the key to the future of NLP. As we share ideas and applications with one another, we stimulate new ideas and applications in other areas. As early NLP influence Gregory Bateson pointed out, "Everything is a metaphor for everything else."

Both the book and the practice groups from which it emerged are the fruits of the sustained vision, sponsorship and efforts of Judith Lowe of PPD Learning. I have known Judith for several decades now and have always been impressed by her level of energy, commitment to excellence and creativity she brings to everything she does. A superb trainer, coach and leader, Judith also inspires others to be proactive and pursue their passion with confidence and creativity. May this book and its authors inspire you to do the same!

Robert Dilts
NLP University
Santa Cruz, California

Foreword by Judith DeLozier

It is a pleasure to write a foreword for this generous contribution to the field of NLP. It rings some echoes of the past. In the eighties John Grinder and I edited a book called Leaves Before the Wind. It was a gathering of articles by people in the field of NLP who were making contributions or breaking new ground. The spirit of the book was to honour the work and commitment of these people to making new applications and for pushing into new territory for the time. It was, at least, my hope that somehow it would set a precedent that would continue. I saw in my dream many volumes of new contributions and new applications that would benefit the whole field of NLP. I wanted the book to honour those contributors who might be missed in the bright light of the gods and goddesses. It is wonderful to see this delightful, rich and diverse offering.

I was moved by the commitment of these individuals who showed up to practise the practice of NLP and through this practice as you will see there emerges both mastery and artistry. I remember the early days of NLP and the amazing energy, curiosity and learning that were sparking to bring some ideas into the world. It was then a generative effort and I can see the beauty of generative effort and individual contribution in this beautiful book. I see these authors as models of inspiration and commitment for us all in the field. They are models of possibility for us all.

I love the diversity of articles and strategies, from leadership to cross species communication, from creativity to negotiations and beyond. There is truly something for all of us to learn regardless of our context of application. The processes offered are thoughtful, full, practical and transformational. They are also evidence based which is key for us NLP folks. Through their work the authors are validating other peoples intuitive processes. I thought that the processes were elegant and they work. I had a friend read over the manuscript and thanked her for making the effort. Her response was, "I am not helping you, and I am being helped." This says a lot. These lovely people are colleagues yes, and many friends as well. They are unique and extremely kind people who I feel that I have walked the walk with for these ten years and more. I feel so honoured to be with them all on the journey. I see each person's passion reflected in their words of wisdom.

Now I feel it is also important to honour PPD Learning and Judith Lowe for creating the space and the focus for this ongoing opportunity to explore deeper and wider into the models, skills and techniques of NLP. Judith Lowe has consistently sought out the edge, she consistently asked us who come to train at PPD Learning to push the edge and develop new ground. She is a creative force for me and a kindred spirit. She is committed to making a difference through PPD Learning and makes a point of sustaining a social contribution through her organization. Again, both Judith Lowe and PPD Learning are great models and serve as inspiration for us all. Judith the catalyst, Judith who takes us to eco-learning.

It is my hope that this book becomes a tradition, a breath of fresh air that comes to us periodically to enliven us all and honour the amazing contributors and contributions.

Thank you all for shining the light and bringing awareness.

Judith Delozier

Contents

Foreword by Robert Dilts 9

Foreword by Judith DeLozier 11

Introduction by Judith Lowe 15

Build Your Resilience *by Muriel McClymont* 19

Negotiation Skills *by Simon Horton* 37

Unravelling Complexities: Tidying up our intimate relationships
by Juliet Grayson 47

Alpha Leadership *by Anne Deering* 59

Exploring Other Worlds *by Dido Fisher* 77

Zen in The Art of The NLP Meta Model *by Judith Lowe* 93

The Five-Minute Coach *by Lynne Cooper* 109

Finding Work Through Relationships *by Christopher Howell* 123

Be More Creative *by Jonathan Goldsmith* 137

Study Skills for All Ages and All Occasions *by Paddy Bergin* 155

NLP in the Wild *by Judith Lowe* 173

Appendix A: Running a Successful Practice Group 187

Appendix B: The PPD Learning 'Introducing NLP' Manual 189

Appendix C: Resources & Bibliography 207

Appendix D: PPD Learning - NLP Training 209

Appendix E: Passion In Action - Social Change with NLP 211

*"In theory there is no difference between theory and practice.
In practice there is."*

Yogi Berra

Welcome to the PPD Learning NLP Practice Group - in a book!

We ran our 'everyone invited' evenings for nearly 10 years at the London University Student's Union just up the road from the British Museum.

The young, lively, multicultural student community there always felt like a perfect setting for us, as the field of NLP was itself created at the University of California, on a student campus at Santa Cruz.

The original NLP research and the development of NLP tools, skills and approaches was carried out there by an informal group of academics and students, led by Richard Bandler and John Grinder. Their intellectual curiosity about learning and change in living systems combined with their behavioural modelling of exceptional therapists, Fritz Perls, Virginia Satir and Milton Erickson, inspired them to create NLP, a new pragmatic model of effective communication and performance.

This behavioural modelling approach and the many innovative techniques for systemic change, problem-solving and effective influence it created, is now practised by millions of people all over the world and is a key part of many professional trainings across multiple application areas.

Our Practice Group sessions in London were fun, friendly and practical. We wanted people to enjoy the evening socially as well as refine and develop their skills and understanding of NLP. We welcomed our own community of students, Practitioners and Master Practitioners, as well as visitors. Often the range of abilities in the room was from beginner through to experienced NLP trainer and coach.

We practise an NLP that promotes emotional and somatic intelligence, integrity and warm heartedness, and in which the results of any NLP process can be publicly tested and evaluated with sensory-based evidence, as the client demonstrates more generative and ecological behavioural choices.

The sessions in this book are mainly a selection from our wonderful special guest evenings. The contributors are all former students and now current friends and colleagues of ours at PPD Learning. Over a period of several years I invited them to bring their specialist NLP application to the practice group.

I hope there's something here for everyone. The applications are for leadership, coaching, negotiation, study skills, networking, relationships, creativity, resilience, use of language and adventures with culture and art. So there's lots to practice and enjoy.

Although all the topics are based in NLP, some of the chapters also contain material from models outside of the field. I hope you find that this works well for your practice group. It shows how experts from within the NLP field are able to use NLP creatively as a fundamental base for innovation into many different areas.

I have included for every chapter, relevant background material, specific steps for exercises and activities, and tips to make the session go well. Also I have attached most of our PPD Learning 'Introducing NLP' manual to help with key models and definitions of NLP that can also be used as handouts in practitioner skills sessions.

As you can tell, I'm very passionate about people continuing to practise their NLP skills alongside and beyond their official training period. Together in a group you can create a golden opportunity for live action, quality feedback, error correction and shared sensory calibration to progress and results.

Now that NLP is also being offered online it seems important to affirm that NLP is based in subtle, intelligent, interactive, embodied behavioural skills. Like a top athlete or musician it's the practice that makes the difference, with the so-called 'ten thousand hours' of quality focus and calibrated improvement over time.

I hope this book contributes to a lifelong learning ethos for practitioners in the NLP field and that the groups and individuals who use it feel encouraged and cheered along their path of learning and development by me and the other contributors.

I look forward to hearing from anyone and everyone who uses this book and wish you much joy from it.

My thanks go to many people. Thank you to Simon Horton and Alex Marshall for running our early practice groups with such great spirit. Thank you to the wonderful contributors to this book for so being so generous with your time and materials – Paddy Bergin, Lynne Cooper, Anne Deering, Dido Fisher, Jonathan Goldsmith, Juliet Grayson, Simon Horton, Christopher Howell and Muriel McClymont.

Thank you of course to all the wonderful and inspirational NLP teachers and trainers at PPD Learning over the years, especially Robert Dilts, Judy DeLozier, John Grinder, Christina Hall, Stephen Gilligan, Charles Faulkner, David Gordon, Julian Russell, Joseph O'Connor and David Gaster.

Thank you to my many wonderful colleagues in the field in the UK for your friendship and support. Thank you to my own dear friends and family too, especially Loretta Loach.

Thank you to everyone at PPD Learning who has supported this project especially Christopher Howell and Jonathan Goldsmith.

Special thanks to Sean Finnan and Lynne Cooper for their last minute comments and corrections, which have made all the difference, and of course very special thanks to Muriel McClymont, without whose drive and leadership we may never have got this far.

Thank you to all our delightful, inspirational NLP students over nearly 30 years.

This is for you!

Judith Lowe

BUILD YOUR RESILIENCE

by
Muriel McClymont

*"I've lived through some
terrible things in my life,
some of which actually happened."*

MARK TWAIN

Biography of Muriel McClymont

Muriel is an experienced coach and trainer. Originally from a senior business background, she has over 20 years experience working with people as a manager, coach and trainer.

Muriel completed her NLP Practitioner at NLPU in Santa Cruz and her Master Practitioner with PPD Learning in London. She has continued to develop her NLP skills at every opportunity ever since, with trainers including Judith Lowe, Robert Dilts, Judy DeLozier and Christina Hall.

In addition to running her own coaching business, where she has a range of private and commercial clients, Muriel is a tutor with the Federation of Entertainment Unions (FEU) Training, where she works with actors, musicians and writers, delivering workshops on topics including Negotiation, Developing Assertiveness, Goal Setting, Motivation, Developing Resilience and Confidence Boosting.

Prior to her career as a coach and trainer she was a Commercial Director in the Facilities Management sector.

Muriel joined the PPD Learning team in 2010 for a short ten-week contract, and has never left!

www.lumiercoaching.co.uk

I work with creative freelancers including actors, musicians and writers, who frequently and routinely have to deal with rejections and disappointments. The only to way to survive in their industries is to learn strategies to develop inner strength and resilience in order to stay motivated for the next opportunity, and the one after that.

These skills and strategies aren't only useful for creative freelancers, they're also invaluable if you work in sales, as a manager, teacher or organise events. Unplanned things happen, clients, customers, pupils and employers become unhappy, and negative feedback, mishaps or disappointments at some point are inevitable. This session is about learning how to deal with the knocks in a way that develops resilience, allows learning to occur and helps people stay resourceful.

Although this is an NLP session I usually deliver it to a non-NLP audience, so rarely mention NLP. That way no-one gets distracted with unfamiliar labels, they just focus on themselves and the experience they are having.

What is Resilience?

When we talk about resilience in the natural world we are usually describing how capable an environment or ecosystem is of recovering after a devastating event such as a flood or fire. Similarly with people, staying resilient is being able to recover your own equilibrium when an event or circumstances has knocked you off course.

All of us face a multitude of challenges in our lives, ranging from minor to devastating. Being resilient is not about being impervious to setbacks, rather it's having an inbuilt pathfinder or compass that keeps bringing us back to a place of balance and resourcefulness.

There are many aspects to resilience but for the purposes of this session I focus on four, which I call the four pillars. I illustrate each one using people who have inspired me with their examples of extreme or super resilience.

The four pillars of resilience

- Taking responsibility

- Having a clear purpose

- Setting manageable goals

- Focusing on what you can do

Taking responsibility

Before Nelson Mandela became the President of South Africa he spent 27 years in prison. In his autobiography, Long Walk to Freedom, he shares his journey from young lawyer, through campaigner and activist, to outstanding statesman. An inspiring read.

He talks about the impact the poem Invictus, by William Ernest Henley, had on him. At the time he read it he was in prison doing hard labour. This poem, including the lines: "I am the master of my fate, I am the Captain of my soul." helped Mandela to understand that regardless of how badly he was treated, no-one could control what he thought, or who he truly was.

What Mandela did next in leading his country through the process of the dissolution of apartheid was incredible.

In terms of resilience, the big understanding was in recognising that even when he couldn't control or change what was happening to him, he could always choose how he *responded* to what happened. How he thought and whether he stayed true to himself was always entirely his responsibility.

Having a clear purpose

Victor Frankl, a psychiatrist and neurologist, spent three years during World War Two as an inmate of concentration camps. His book, Man's Search for Meaning, is an account of how he used this horrendous experience to observe and learn what made the difference between the people who did and didn't survive, amongst those not deliberately or randomly killed.

Frankl learned that survival did not necessarily depend on how fit or able people were. According to him, physically strong individuals would sometimes get rapidly sick, weaken and die unexpectedly, while some frail individuals seemed surprisingly able to withstand the cruel hardships.

Frankl observed that people with a deep and personal purpose somehow fared better. This purpose could be to see family or loved ones again, to finish writing a book, or a determination to share their experiences with the world. Those who didn't have something or someone to live for were far more likely to give up mentally, and then deteriorate physically.

In our lives, where most of our challenges and setbacks are less extreme, the same principles exist. Having a clear purpose is very powerful and makes prioritising much easier. It's a great foundation from which to make difficult decisions, conquer setbacks and to stay creative when overcoming difficulties.

Setting manageable goals

The story of Joe Simpson and his climbing partner Simon Yates and their disastrous climbing experience in the Andes is captured in Joe Simpson's book and the documentary film, Touching the Void.

While climbing together in a remote part of the Andes, Joe slipped, shattering his tibia and knee joint. With no available rescue service, Simon attempted to lower Joe down the side of the mountain. They miscalculated their descent plan and Joe was left suspended over the cliff attached to Simon at night and in a storm.

Simon had to take the awful decision to cut the rope and save himself, as both would have died had he not. Joe, already seriously injured fell 150 feet. Simon searched for him the following morning before heading back to their camp assuming he was probably dead.

In spite of his injuries, Joe crawled five miles over three days back to the camp, with no food and little water. He tells how overwhelming it was for him to think about how far the camp was, so he didn't consider that. Instead he picked a rock, 10 metres away, and gave himself 20 minutes to reach it. Then he picked another rock, and another 20 minutes, and so on and so on. He rewarded himself with a sip of water after achieving each small target.

Joe's survival is a testament to his exceptional determination and bravery. He achieved it by setting small, achievable goals.

The motivation for Joe was clear: had he not taken each painful step he would have died. Most of us are lucky enough not to experience such a motivation, however it's good to be reminded that when a task is overwhelming, it may be time to break it down and identify smaller chunks or a first step. Then just do it, without consciously thinking about the whole picture all the time.

Focusing on what you can do

Martine Wright was running a bit late for work on 7 July 2005 after celebrating the award of the 2012 Olympics to London the night before. She got a later tube than usual and sat opposite one of the London underground bombers. Martine was one of the last people to be rescued that day, having lost 80% of her blood and both of her legs. She talks about how, after her recovery, she tried to resume her life as it had been prior to the bombing, but there were too many things she couldn't do as she'd done them before.

Martine's response was to look for new things she could only do without legs! She had an opportunity to play sitting volleyball, loved it and was good at it. She became a member of the British Sitting Volleyball Team. In 2012 Martine represented her country, competing as part of the 2012 Paralympic sitting volleyball team.

Martine has actually said that she considers herself lucky to have been through her ordeal. In the process of her own recovery she saw and experienced many kindnesses in people, and has since had the opportunity to contribute herself in ways she most likely would not have done had she not been injured. Representing Great Britain in 2012 meant a great deal to her.

In exceptional circumstances Martine managed to focus on what she *could* do, and took the opportunities when they came along. Many people would have got stuck at "Why me?" and, "Look what I can't do." Instead, Martine managed to take an inspiringly positive path through this awful experience.

The shift from focusing on what she couldn't do to what she could, was the difference that made the difference for Martine.

These are just a few of the examples I could give and I'm sure you can think of many of your own, but I find it very inspiring to consider just what a difference resilient thinking can make, even in seemingly hopeless environments. Of course that's not to belittle or undermine the lesser challenges that we all experience, rather that if it's possible to do it in extremis, it feels much more achievable for the rest of us.

Outcomes for the session

This whole session embodies the NLP presupposition that we have all the resources we need. I initially set up some framing around how we are all capable of being resilient. I work with the group to help them get a sense of their resilience. We *are* all resilient, we just sometimes need to remember and reconnect with that knowledge. The idea is to make it feel easily achievable by anyone, which it is.

The exercises are designed to create trigger words, images, connections and feelings, called anchors in NLP, for the desired state of resilience. We can then use this to build a stronger resource state, before transferring it to situations where more resilience is wanted, known in NLP as 'mapping across'. (There is more detailed information on anchors and mapping across in the appendices.)

My introduction to the session goes something like this:

We all experience setbacks in our lives and career. Avoiding them isn't possible. Learning how to handle them more effectively absolutely is.

Striving to resolve setbacks is a natural drive. We are born programmed to focus on getting fed, learning to communicate and walk. No toddler sits on the ground focusing on how hard it is to walk, they just find the necessary carpet, table or toy they need to pull themselves up on and have another go.

Feeling helpless and stuck is an understandable, but less helpful, survival response. Learning to recognise this stuckness as a signal to engage alternative strategies can allow this to become a platform from which you can build and structure more resourceful responses, using the four pillars of resilience detailed above.

This session is designed to help you access your sense of resilience, and to offer additional tools and strategies to help develop more resilient responses as you meet your own challenges.

How do you deal with setbacks?

How we deal with setbacks is largely down to how we think about them, the meanings we apply and the consequences we imagine.

Setbacks range from inconvenient to catastrophic; for the purposes of this session I would encourage participants to choose something around a 3 or 4 in a scale of 1-10, where 0 is 'inconvenient' and 10 is 'catastrophic'.

I often work with people who have to bid, apply or audition for every piece of work they get. For such groups I use an example of losing work. In a practice group this would not be appropriate; for many people their jobs are tied to their identity, so losing work would be a 9 or 10 and not a useful premise to work with. So it's important to develop examples that are appropriate to the group, for example, being late for an important appointment, embarrassing yourself in front of your new boss or upsetting a friend.

Lets take the example of being late for an important meeting. If we step back from that, by which I mean take ourselves emotionally out of the situation so we can see it from the position of an observer - what in NLP we call dissociated - we can consider this situation unemotionally. The facts are, you should be somewhere else, but you are stuck on a train, car or plane that's delayed.

To help disassociate people from their negative experiences, when I say, "step back," I emphasise this by physically stepping back to give an additional visual cue to help them disassociate. If people choose a significant challenge, it can be harder for them to dissociate, which is why we suggest a score of 3-4.

There are many ways to react when things don't go to plan, some more useful than others. The following options for this scenario offer just some of the reactions available ranging from making the best of it, making sure it doesn't happen again, and of course, there's always a downwards spiral!

Option 1 Come fully into the present and accept the situation. Then consider what to do about it. Is it possible to send a message or call? Is there work you were going to do together that you could start to work on now, so if the meeting goes ahead anyway you can still add your thoughts later?

If neither of those are possible, is there something else of value you can do to make good use of the time? You can always explain later. Whether that explanation will be good enough or not may be a consequence you have to deal with, but you can't do anything about that right now.

Option 2 Focus on the future and make a list of all the things you could do differently next time. Maybe you could have made a contingency plan, or just left earlier. Identify a range of possibilites and be happy in the knowledge that this situation is unlikely to happen again. You could also then do option 1 or option 3.

Option 3 Slip into a passive mode, where you take self reproach to extremes and start to search for your personal flaws which 'must' have caused this situation. Start to scan your entire history of negative situations and search for evidence to confirm that you are 'helpless', 'worthless' or 'useless'. Then you can feel really, really bad about it!

How you react in this situation is a factor of focus, attitude and habit. It's also a choice point. Becoming more resilient is about making the constructive options your first choice.

I like to use exaggeration to get people laughing at some of the more extreme reactions they might have. I particularly ham up option 3. I have certainly been known to have taken this route in my past and I'm guessing, by the laughs it gets, that I'm not alone. Laughing at unhelpful strategies we've used in the past helps re-code those memories and diminishes their power as automatic responses in the future.

Being Un-resilient

How do people manage to *not* be resilient? Some imagine failing catastrophically or being publically humiliated. Maybe it feels like it's all just too hard, and therefore not even worth trying.

Others develop very complex patterns of thinking that allow them to reliably spiral into gloom and despair whenever they experience the smallest setback.

If you are good at giving up then you already have all the right skills for building resilience - you're just pointing your thoughts and imagination the wrong way.

The Antidote

I use a lot of reframing in this section to demonstrate that what people have been seeing as a problem is actually a resource. I also continue to work on ways to help people disassociate from their problem states.

If you recognise that you sometimes use unhelpful strategies when setbacks occur, then congratulate yourself on having some great skills of focus and creative thinking. Now imagine how powerful those skills would be if they were turned around and used in a positive way.

In order to catastrophise an event, you have to run a sequence of movies - in your head - of escalating negative consequences, until you imagine your entire life crumbling around you. If you get really good at this, missing a bus can result in seeing yourself as homeless and all alone.

Now imagine what it would be like if you replace those negative movies with ones of you taking this setback in your stride, running alternative scenes of new possible opportunities appearing from unexpected quarters, and seeing yourself benefiting from what just occurred. Feels a lot different, doesn't it?

All the same skills and strategy, just used in a different direction.

A good way to feel overwhelmed is to imagine obstacles so vast that overcoming them seems impossible. When someone is feeling overwhelmed, they often lean back as if being intimidated by their own internal pictures.

Moving from overwhelmed to resourceful involves finding ways to scale down the problem. If you are able to create great big pictures and make them loom over you, you are also capable of pushing them away and shrinking them. The NLP terminology for this is using the submodalities (qualities of the representation) to change how an experience makes you feel. (See appendix)

There's often also an issue with the chunk size you are working with. If you are working on a goal that just feels too big, you can chunk it down by considering what five things have to happen to achieve it, and then break each of those five things down in the same way. Eventually you will identify actions that you can do right now. As soon as you can start to take action you move from stuck to active, or overwhelmed to resourceful.

Rather than focusing on the problem, think about what you can do. If you miss a train, there is no point thinking about the train that just left. How can you find out where and when to catch the next one? Many of us waste a lot of time concentrating on the problem, when we could be focusing on the solution. Same skills, different direction.

Instead of thinking your whole life hinges on one event, remember other times in your life when you had that thought and it turned out not to be the case. Recognise that your life and career have developed as an accumulation of effort, developed skills and experience. Know that other opportunities will arise. It's the flip side of the 'lucky break'. People usually spend years being in the right place at the right time before they have their so-called lucky break.

Remember too that so-called setbacks can become narrow escapes. As a career coach I've worked with many people initially devastated by being made redundant, who subsequently come to realise that it was the best thing that ever happened to them. Also, remember the earlier example of Martine Wright, who came to consider losing her legs in the London bombing as something that ultimately changed her life for the better.

> *"I've lived through some terrible things in my life,*
>
> *some of which actually happened"*
>
> Mark Twain

Menu of key tools, models & skills

- Presupposition - We all have all the resources we need

- Perceptual positions

- Anchoring/Building anchors

- Mapping across

- Reframing
- Association / Disassociation

Exercises and Activities

You can do some or all of these exercises. Exercise 1 can be done on its own, followed by exercise 2 and 3, or just with exercise 3 if time is short.

Exercise 1 - Finding your own resilience

Work in pairs. Allow 20 minutes each way for this exercise, with around 10-20 minutes to feed back to the group. If people are given sufficient time they will get a real sense of their resilience. I've often seen people surprised that they have this core resource.

You may find it helpful to create a handout from the table in the exercise.

Instructions

Pick a time when you were resilient, and work out how exactly you did this. This might have been a physical experience such as completing a crossword, passing an exam, pursuing a career break or achieving a challenge you set yourself. Take turns to interview each other using the questions below and capture the key elements of the strategies you used.

As the coach it's important to look out for the physiology of the state the coachee is accessing. What gestures are they using? Are they symmetrical? What is their posture like? Are there changes in skin colour or demeanour? It may be useful to feed some of this back to bring it to the coachee's attention.

What did you focus on?	
How did you solve any problems that arose?	
What did you tell yourself about this?	
What motivated you to do it?	
How did you feel?	

At the end of each turn, make sure the coachee identifies a word, symbol, gesture, posture or colour that represents their resilience.

These questions help to establish whether participants are internally or externally focused in this state. They help them to unconsciously access the modalities and submodalities of their resilience, and their motivation strategies.

By modality I mean the visual, auditory or kinaesthetic elements of their representation. The submodalities are the key variable qualities of those representations, such as the size or brightness of images, volume or quality of sounds and the position and strength of sensations and feelings.

Accessing the information in this way helps the coachee build up a fuller representation of this state, and makes it easier for them to identify and strengthen it as a resource. (For more information on modalities and sub modalities see the appendices)

In the feedback session I would draw out all of these elements and compare and contrast this to the alternative physiology, focus and internal chatter of the non-resilient states we discussed earlier.

Next, I work with the group to reinforce the symbol, word, sensation or picture that individuals have identified to represent their resilient resource, and talk them through making this stronger and more accessible as an anchor for them to take away.

I check that everyone has a clear representation, help anyone who doesn't, then ask them to focus and get a really strong sense of their own resilience as they have chosen to represent it.

*I might say something like, "Think of your symbol, word, feeling, physiology or picture that represents your resilience now, and get a full sense of this state, where you know you have all the skills and strategies you need. Take a moment to really enjoy what it feels like to know that you can keep going, whatever happens, finding routes around obstacles, and solutions to any problems that arise, to continue to work towards your goals now... and if you would like to... allow it to expand and grow stronger and more powerful... until you **know** that you can access this resource whenever you want to, today, tomorrow or in the weeks, months or years ahead."*

Exercise 2 - Borrowing your hero's resilience

Work in pairs. Allow 10-15 minutes each way for this one.

To demonstrate this exercise I use my impression of Jack Nicholson in some of his more benign roles where he just oozes confidence when he walks into a room. I choose Nicholson because with his confidence and forceful personality he is the polar opposite to me in many ways. So when I stand in front of the group and adopt his posture and swagger, and then look around the room with his slightly superior, semi-aggressive gaze, it nicely illustrates what I want the group to do. And it usually gets a laugh! It changes completely how I feel inside and I share that with the group too.

*I use Nicholson as an example to illustrate that when looking for someone who has the resources you want, you don't have to choose someone you admire every aspect of. I can think of many aspects of Jack Nicholson that I have no desire to experience, so when I try on his confidence that is **all** I am accessing. This has to feel ecological for people, so it's important to explain that you are only going to borrow the bits you like and admire. You leave all the rest behind completely undisturbed.*

If I were to choose a true hero of mine, I would opt for Gill, a woman I've worked closely with over the last five years, whose resilience throughout a number of major life changes has been inspirational to me. However, as no-one in the group is likely to know her, this would not be as good, or funny, a demo.

Instructions

Working in pairs, guide each other through this process. Think of someone you admire for their resilience. This can be someone you know or someone famous. Imagine what it's like being them. Use a marker on the floor and 'step into their shoes'; really take the time to experience what their resilience feels like.

It's important to use their posture and gestures. See the world through their eyes, hear through their ears and feel the world through their skin. The coachee should talk to the coach about their resilience, *as the person they are modelling*, so the coach should make sure the coachee uses the word "I", not "they". Stay in character so you can capture the real essence of this state as your hero.

The coach should help the coachee to be clear about what elements of this person's resilience they want to take away and 'borrow', and separate that out from the rest which can be 'left behind'. Now find a symbol, word or colour that represents this resilient state for you, make it really strong and clear and make a note of it.

Exercise 3 - Building resilience

In pairs, allow 20-30 minutes each way for this exercise.

Make sure you explain this one carefully as people with not much NLP experience may find this confusing. I use a diagram on a flipchart, have it in the handout and pace it out physically while explaining it at least twice.

Emphasise that the role of the coach is to support the process by prompting with the words, symbols and physiology identified in the earlier exercises (the anchors) and holding the space to let each step integrate for the coachee. The coach should be constantly checking that what the coachee is saying is being backed up by their physiology. If not, they can use the anchors to help prompt them as appropriate.

Instructions

Do this in pairs, taking turns to be coach and coachee. The coach is there to guide and remind the coachee of the process and to prompt the coachee with reminders of the anchors identified in earlier exercises, especially if the coach calibrates that they are not fully accessing their anchored states.

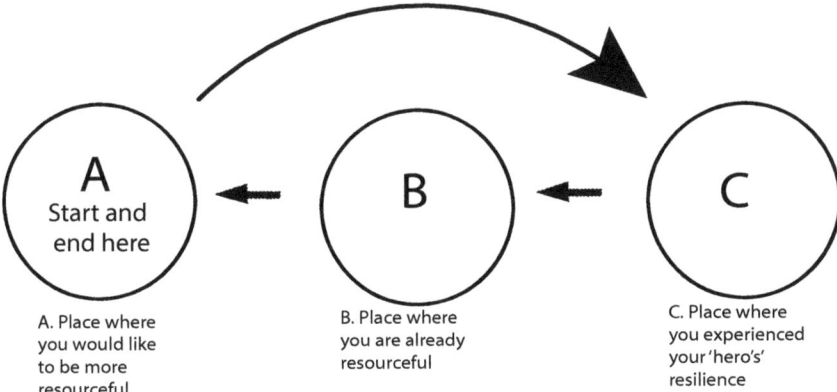

A
Start and
end here

B

C

A. Place where
you would like
to be more
resourceful

B. Place where
you are already
resourceful

C. Place where
you experienced
your 'hero's'
resilience

Mark out three spaces on the floor as in the diagram above.

Position A A situation where you would like to experience more resilience.

Position B A context in which you are already resilient – *the example you found in exercise 1.*

Position C Your resilience 'hero' space – *that you identified in exercise 2.*

The coachee steps into position A and identifies somewhere they would like to be more resilient, thinking about it only long enough to get a light sense of it.

The coach now guides the coachee to move from that space, leaving all that belongs there in position A, and walk to position C.

We are trying to achieve three clean states, so it's important for the coach to monitor posture and body language to check that the coachee has fully shaken off each state. You certainly don't want them taking any of the problem state into the newly defined resource states.

As coach you are calibrating that the coachee has left the state fully behind in the allocated spaces, If you think this has not happened you may need to use a 'break state' question such as, "Do you like the carpet?" to bring them 'back into the room'. (A break state question is just as it sounds - ask the coachee something specific so they have to focus elsewhere to answer, thus changing state)

The coachee now steps in to position C and accesses the resilience resource captured from the 'hero' in exercise 2. The coach should give the coachee a moment to access that resource again prompting with their symbol, word or picture if required. Then, taking only the desired resources from that person, the coachee steps into position B, the coachee's own resilient state.

The coach holds the space while the coachee integrates this new resource with their own resilient resources, creating a new expanded state. The coach should watch the coachee closely and calibrate when this has happened. Once the coach feels that the coachee has this new, integrated resource, he or she asks the coachee to step into Position A, where they would like more resilience.

The coach should allow space and time for integration and processing to take place when the coachee steps into position A. The coach should again carefully focus on the coachee, calibrating whether they need any verbal support, or are busy processing. Once the coachee has integrated it all, the coach can ask about what changes the coachee noticed in A, or what felt different.

When wrapping up the session it's important to pull out success stories from the session to help reinforce the process for everyone. Discussing what happened and the details of how people made it work for them, helps the whole group to get clearer about their own experiences.

Final Notes

It's good to maintain a really playful attitude with this practice group; participants will access these states much more easily if they have fun with it.

For me, the most important thing I want people to take away is that they have lots of untapped resources within themselves.

I want people to be aware of how much choice they have over how they feel.

Ideally, participants will leave the workshop feeling resourceful and resilient.

Building resilience is a matter of developing skills, capacity and understanding of how to make more useful choices. This grows with time and experience. The content of this session is something to take away, carry forward and continue to develop as part of the process of your developing resilience.

Negotiation Skills

by

Simon Horton

"Everything that involves other people involves negotiation; get good at negotiation, get good at life."

Biography of Simon Horton

Simon is one of the world's leading Negotiation Skills trainers, having taught hostage negotiators, senior purchasing officers for some of the largest global manufacturing companies and solicitors at the most prestigious law firms in the world.

He is a Visiting Lecturer at Imperial College, University of London, and has worked with many tier one banks, pharmaceutical and oil companies.

He is the author of the Amazon bestseller, Negotiation Mastery. In his spare time, he is a trapeze artist and used to perform as a stand-up comedian.

www.negotiation-mastery.com

I've been teaching negotiation skills for over 10 years now and one thing that has struck me is that it is absolutely core to everything we do. Anything we do that involves other people, involves negotiation... and everything we do involves other people.

I teach lawyers, sales-people, managers and students; I coach people looking for pay-rises, people getting divorced, parents wanting their kids to study harder. Whether at work or at home or with friends, we are negotiating. We even negotiate with ourselves! I've come to the conclusion that if you get good at negotiation, you get good at life.

And interestingly, the same principles and the same negotiation structures and techniques apply to a negotiation with your child to tidy the room as to a multi-billion dollar corporate mergers & acquisitions deal.

NLP brings so much to negotiation; there is hardly a pre-supposition or a technique that doesn't apply. So what to cover in a "NLP and negotiation" workshop? Well, with 'context = everywhere', and 'content = everything', your main issue is going to be what not to include.

So this chapter will focus on a couple of core NLP techniques, the well-formed outcome and perceptual positions, and will relate them to the negotiation context.

Outcome for the session

The outcome for this session is for students to go away with methods to achieve the best deal they can from any negotiation in a manner that is sustainable, whether it is a commercial or legal transaction, or simply one with a friend or family member.

Menu of key tools

- Well-formed outcome

- Perceptual positions

Exercises and Activities

Exercise 1 - What can NLP bring to...?

A fast-forward exploration of what NLP can bring to negotiation, thereby deconstructing it from an NLP framework, immediately giving people a better grasp on a subject often considered mysterious, and giving them possibilities for improving.

Allow 20 minutes for this group discussion. The tutor captures answers on a flip-chart.

A great place to start any practice group is to ask the question "What can NLP bring to...?" the particular topic of that event, in this instance, negotiation. As well as reminding the audience of all of the different elements to NLP, it gives a framework for understanding that subject from an NLP perspective. They quickly realise that almost everything in NLP has an input into negotiation and that, therefore, they are perhaps better at it than they thought and have routes forward for becoming even better.

You can also bring home to people the pervasiveness of negotiation by asking them for examples of negotiations in their life. They will find it very easy to identify many and very quickly they will come to the realisation that we are negotiating everywhere. This, in itself, is often quite a powerful insight for people.

Exercise 2 - Well-formed outcome

In this exercise students will learn the value of having a well-formed outcome in a negotiation. (See appendix.) They will also learn some variations on the concept that are specifically relevant to negotiating.

Working in pairs, allow 15 minutes to introduce the topic, 15 minutes for the exercise (7.5 minutes each way) and 15 minutes for discussion afterwards: a total of 45 minutes.

Instructions

1.   Introduce the topic of win-win. How do we achieve win-win? Well, it's your

win and their win. What NLP technique does "your win" conjure? Using the well-formed outcomes model discuss how it relates to getting your deal.

2. Discuss the following questions:

- Ultimately, what do you really want beyond this deal?

- Therefore, what do you want from this deal?

- What is your Maximum Plausible Position?

- What is your Best Alternative To a Negotiated Agreement (BATNA)?

- What are the different variables involved?

3. Activity: delegates work in pairs, applying the above questions to negotiations they are involved in. 7.5 mins each way.

4. Discussion of activity.

Notes:

The first question will be familiar to NLP'er's as an example of chunking up. From a negotiation point of view, it is very important because it puts this particular deal in context. Many deals that become deadlocked can be resolved at the level of the bigger picture. I worked with the purchasing department of a large manufacturing company and the very first question on their requisition order form was "What is the mission of this company?". Starting with this question in mind means that everything else about the deal will be aligned with the company's strategic direction.

In fact, it is the first principle cited in Fisher and Ury's classic, "Getting to Yes", the book that has sold 8 million copies and has become the de facto standard in the field. In their words, "Focus on interests, not positions"; translated to English, it says it is a mistake to get entrenched in fixed positions like "I'll never pay more than £1000". Instead, think of your bigger picture and how you can best achieve that. It's not about winning a battle, its about winning the war.

The second question is the classic well-formed outcome which NLP'ers will know. Then the next two questions address the range of possible outcomes you may get from the deal.

It is often asked whether you should be the first to mention a figure in a deal or not and, although the old orthodoxy was always to wait until you hear the other party's position, it is now considered best practice to open the talks yourself. Research has shown that the first figure mentioned is likely to affect the final result – so be the person who mentions the first figure - and make sure the figure is a good one for you! That is, start with your Maximum Plausible Position – the highest figure you can mention that you can plausibly justify. It isn't that you will always get this figure but it is a good place to start.

I believe you should be ambitious and optimistic with your plans. Set your expectations high and you are more likely to achieve them. So I think it is even worth considering other things you would like to get, above and beyond your Maximum Plausible Position. Things that aren't plausible at all! But if you don't think about them, you definitely wont get them; do and you just might.

Your Best Alternative To a Negotiated Agreement (BATNA) is effectively your Plan B – where would you be left if this deal fell through – and it is a very important concept in negotiations for a number of reasons. For a start, it gives you a very clear idea about when you should walk away from the deal. Often people have a bottom-line ("I won't sell for anything less than £2000") but they usually come to this figure from gut-feel. Your BATNA is a real-world guide to your bottom-line – if you are being offered one penny more than your BATNA, take it; one penny less, walk away.

The corollary of this is that you should work hard to develop a strong BATNA. The success of any particular deal is a function of the BATNA – the better your Plan B, the more confident you will feel in asking for more from this deal. The classic example is when you are haggling over the vase in the marketplace. As soon as you start to leave the shop to go to the one next door, almost certainly selling an identical vase, the price drops.

There is a saying in negotiations that the deal goes to the person most willing to walk away. This isn't always true but it is a helpful guideline. On the other hand, you don't want to bluff. It can be very embarrassing if you start to walk out the door and they say, "Ok, goodbye!" So always make sure you have a strong BATNA.

Then, if the other party are not offering you more than this, be prepared to go elsewhere. Before you do, tell them of your alternative – it gives them a last chance to up their price.

The final question to discuss is to identify the different variables involved in the negotiation. These variables are any elements that can be brought into the conversation. For example, if you are buying a house, you may think the negotiation will only be around the price but there are other elements to be considered. Is it a cash payment or mortgaged? Is there a chain or not? How quickly can they complete? Will they leave the furniture and fittings? Will they extend the lease for you? Will it include the parking space or not? Can you move in before completion? Can they stay and rent it after completion?

The point is that the more variables you can identify, the greater chance of horse-trading, the greater chance of finding a mutually beneficial solution. Ideally you find something that is easy for you to give but valuable for them and you swap that for something easy for them to give but valuable to you. Now everyone is better off.

Bringing in different variables is another great way of getting around deadlock. If there is only one dimension to the deal, eg, price, it is easy to reach an impasse. Any penny I gain will necessarily be at your expense, any penny you gain will necessarily be at my expense. It becomes an arm-wrestle and frequently ends up in stalemate. Bring in other variables, though, and you have ways of getting around the impasse.

Exercise 3 - Second Position

In this exercise students learn the value of viewing a negotiation from the other party's perspective.

Working in pairs, allow 10 minutes to introduce the topic, 20 minutes for the exercise (10 minutes each way) and 15 minutes for the discussion: 45 minutes in total.

Instructions:

1. Discuss the following questions:

   • What is going on in your world?

   • Ultimately, what do you really want beyond this deal?

- Therefore, what do you want from this deal?

- What is your Maximum Plausible Position?

- What is your Best Alternative To a Negotiated Agreement (BATNA)?

- What are the different variables involved?

- Where is a possible win-win solution?

- What helpful advice would you give to Person A?

2. Activity: In pairs, person A thinks of a negotiation they are involved in and steps into the shoes of the counterparty, seeing the deal from their perspective. Person B asks the above questions which Person A answers, *as their negotiating counterparty.*

3. Discussion of activity.

Notes:

Having addressed "your win", we now look at "their win", using the second position perspective to gain useful insights. Depending on the time available and the level of experience of the delegates, you may or may not wish to do a demo but the important point is that the delegate really steps into the shoes of their negotiating counterparty to understand their perspective.

The first question is very general and should be answered in the broadest sense – work, family, hobbies, environment and so on. It all provides interesting insight into the world of their counterparty.

Then, with two exceptions at the end, the rest of the questions are exactly the same as those in the previous activity. They ask "What do you really want?" in order to understand the other person's bigger picture. Then chunk down to what they want from this particular deal, using the well-formed criteria.

Consider, also their Maximum Plausible Position and, just as with yourself, be ambitious and optimistic for them. This is counter to old school negotiation approaches which urge you to restrict what the other party gets. If you are creative and can think of a way of helping your counterparty get a good deal, perhaps a better deal than they had expected, you will have an ally for life. That is good.

Of course, it should not be in a way that harms you, remember we are talking win-win, not lose-win.

Their range is important too so if you can identify their BATNA, you will have a very good idea of what they should accept as a deal. That said, don't expect your counterparty to have done the thinking, so if you are offering more than their BATNA and they still aren't happy, you may have to point out the situation.

The variables in the negotiation are likely to be the same from both perspectives but sometimes asking "your counterparty" (in second position), you get new answers that you had not thought of before.

The final two questions are very powerful, especially the last one. By asking "your counterparty" for a possible win-win and helpful advice, you should get quite interesting insight into a solution.

Further Tips

So to make sure you enjoy this practice group, smile, listen, make jokes and laugh at everyone else's. And brush your hair.

Unravelling Complexities: Tidying up our intimate relationships

by
Juliet Grayson

"You meet someone and you're sure you were lovers in a past life. After two weeks with them, you realize why you haven't kept in touch for the last two thousand years."

AL CLEATHEN

Biography of Juliet Grayson

When Juliet Grayson first studied NLP in 1991 it was life changing for her, and she became a passionate advocate. She dedicated the next ten years to getting NLP 'into the muscle' and completed several Practitioner and six Master Practitioner courses.

She now spends half her time working as a sex and relationship therapist and the rest of her time travelling - running ongoing personal development groups across the UK, teaching other therapists about working with couples and running corporate workshops on communication.

She recently co-founded StopSO, the Specialist Treatment Organisation for the Prevention of Sexual Offending, which offers anyone in the UK who feels at risk of sexual offending or re-offending the opportunity to have therapy with someone trained and willing to work with them.

www.therapyandcounselling.co.uk/diary.htm
www.interactiontraining.co.uk
www.stopso.org.uk
www.sexuallyinappropriatebehaviour.org

I think everyone deserves to have a good enough relationship and a good enough sex life. I guess you could say that this is my passion, helping people to connect to one another, and also to connect to their own deeper selves. This requires an acceptance of all of who we are, and is underpinned by honesty, authenticity and self awareness. NLP has been invaluable in my work as a sex and relationship therapist. If I am honest, when I came across NLP it transformed my own life. So I am delighted to be asked to share two exercises that might help people in a practice group. Naturally I am drawn to include something that helps with intimate relationships.

The first exercise is about complex equivalence. This is where two or more experiences are talked about as if they were equivalent. It happens when a set of behaviours equals a label. For example, because Simon brings Sally flowers on Friday (*behaviour*) then Sally knows he loves her (*label*). If Simon doesn't bring Sally flowers on Friday, then to her, it means he no longer loves her! Of course this is an irrational assumption as there may be many other reasons why Simon didn't bring flowers. For example, he may have been busy and worked late, or the flower shop may have been shut. However, because in Sally's map of the world there is an unconscious connection between these behaviours and the label of being loved, Sally feels wounded.

In my therapy with couples, I see people putting in enormous amounts of effort to express their love for their partner, and yet the partner may not recognise how much they are loved. This is because the love is being expressed in ways that they may not label as loving. I remember John and Sheila - John often looked at Sheila with an expression of absolute love in our sessions, but Sheila didn't seem to notice. Exasperated, John asked me 'What more do I have to do to show my love?' I asked him 'How do you show your love currently. What do you do?' He paused a moment and said: "Well I mow the lawn. I hate it, and the only reason I do it is that she likes the garden to look nice". Sheila's face was a picture. When I asked what was going on for her she told me she was amazed and appalled. She didn't really want John mowing the lawn. They could pay someone to do that! What Sheila wanted was some attention. A hug at the end of the day would be the one thing that would mean more to her than him mowing the lawn for a whole summer. Now it was John's turn to be astonished. And pleased, because hugging her was going to be a whole lot easier than mowing the lawn.

This often happens. Person A is putting masses of effort in to the relationship, but not in the place where it has an impact on their partner. When I see couples doing this, I suggest that they get really clear about where the effort is actually wanted, and then they can each refine what they do. Often they can do less and yet it will have much more impact, because it is what their partner really wants, and so it 'lands'. Our first exercise explores this issue.

The second exercise looks at the links between your intimate relationship and your childhood experiences. Negative anchors, set up in childhood, can get triggered and fired by your current partner. If this is not recognised it can create difficulties leading to misunderstandings and hurt on both sides. In such cases it can be hard to work out what is causing so much pain, because the distress is out of proportion to the current behaviour. This is one of the major indicators that a childhood issue is getting re-triggered.

Outcomes for the session

To explore what makes you feel loved, and what makes your partner feel loved.

To check what anchors from childhood relationships may be recreated or triggered in your current relationship,

Menu of key tools, models & skills

- Map of the world

- Complex equivalence

- Perceptual positions

- Spatial sorting

- Anchoring

- Rapport

Exercises and Activities

In the following exercises where I refer to a partner, this could be a current sexual partner, an ex-partner, or a close but not intimate friendship.

Exercise 1 - Being Loved

Outcomes:

- To develop your self-awareness

- To clarify your complex equivalences around being loved

- To consider your partner's complex equivalences

- To identify areas where you are not getting your own needs met

- In relation to your partner, to consider where you are wasting energy and could utilise your energy in a more productive way

- To recognise how different our needs are

Work initially on your own, and then in groups of 3-4 for a discussion. The whole exercise will take approximately 30-40 minutes. You will need a sheet of A4 paper and a pen

Instructions:

1. Draw a line horizontal line across the middle of a piece of paper and a vertical one, again across the middle. This will give boxes. For clarity, I am going to call you A. I am going to ask you to think about another person who is in your life - this could be a sexual partner, an ex-partner or a close (but not intimate) friend. I am going to call this person B.

2. In the top left hand box, answer this question. 'As A, what do you want B to do that would let you know that you are loved by them?' Make a list of all the behaviours that you would like someone who loves you to do for you, with you, or to you. This might include things such as touch (hug me, hold my hand), words (tell me you love me), actions (mow the lawn for me, bring me a cup of tea in the morning, buy me flowers, dress up when we go out together), spending quality time together, etc. This is your 'wish list'. Allow about 5 minutes for this.

3. In the top right hand box, write the answer to this question: 'What does B actually do, that B thinks will make you feel loved?' Allow about 3-5 minutes for this.

4. In the bottom left hand box, write the answer to: 'What do you, A, do for B to let them know that you love them?' Allow about 3-5 minutes for this.

5. Now, step into your B's shoes, and let yourself really take on their way of thinking, feeling, their beliefs and attitudes and even their physiology. Answer this question as if you were B. 'From your perspective as B, what would you like A to do for you, that would make you feel loved?' Allow about 3-5 minutes for this.

6. Having completed this exercise, spend a few moments thinking through what you have learnt, about your own needs and wants, and your partner's.

7. It is very interesting to compare the top left box, with the bottom left box. What you want from B, and what you do for B. Are there any similarities between what you want and what you do?

8. Looking at the top left and the top right boxes: How fully are you getting your needs met? How fully are you meeting your partner's?

9. Finally, compare the top right box with the bottom right box: what does B do for you, and what does B actually want?

10. In 3's have a discussion to share learnings and insights. Using 3rd position, (as well as 1st and 2nd), think about what changes or amendments might enhance your relationship. 10-15 minutes.

As A, what do you want B to do, that would let you know you are loved by them?	What does B actually do that B thinks will make you feel loved?
What do you, A, do for B to let them know that you love them?	As B, what would you like A to do for you that would make you feel loved?

Further Thoughts

- Something I have observed is that often we give others what we most want ourselves. Is this true for you (or your partner) in any way? Have a look at your reflections on (7) and (9) to see if this is true for you or your partner.

- It is interesting to ask your partner to do this exercise, and then compare notes with them to check how well you understand their needs. Did B actually want what you thought they wanted? What do they want but are not currently getting? Is that something that it would be easy to give them or do for them?

- Sometimes our partner wants something we are not willing to give. Jane was living with John, who loves football, but Jane didn't enjoy watching sport. It would be hard for Jane to go to every match through the season. In this situation I advise clients to get clear for themselves about their complex equivalence for being loved and to share those with their partner (don't expect them to guess and to mind read, it is wiser and simpler to tell them). Then let your partner choose the behaviours that are relatively easy for them, and meaningful for you. This means their efforts will be in the areas that make a difference to you and that more of your needs will get met. Likewise, put your efforts where they will have the least cost to you and the most impact on your partner.

Exercise 2a - Cleaning Up Relationships

In the following exercise, when I refer to parents, this could be birth parents, adoptive parents, stepparents, grandparents or caregivers. It is the people who were most influential when you were a child. Usually it would be one or two people, though it could be three or four, for example if your parents divorced and both of them re-married or found new partners.

Outcomes:

- To explore and recognise possible patterns between your parents and partner

- To 'clean up' the relationship with your partner by retracting negative anchors

- To see your partner 'afresh', and remove hypersensitive 'hot buttons'

Working in pairs, allow 20-40 minutes per person. You will need post-its, a pen, tissues and some space.

This exercise uses spatial sorting to create spaces for reflection and insight. It is based on the work of Al Pesso, the co-founder of Pesso Boyden System Psychomotor and relates to aspects of the NLP process of Re-imprinting and also Virginia Satir's family therapy work. In this exercise the coach guides the client through the process.

Instructions The Coach Gives To The Client

1. Find a space in the room for you to explore the current situation and the past. We will call this space (i), and it should be a space that is neutral, where you can reflect. Place a post-it note with your name on to mark this space. You may sit or stand.

2. Create a separate space for your partner, ex-partner, or friend (ii). Write their name on a post-it note and place it to mark the space. Describe the characteristics of your partner, as seen from your perspective.

3. Think about the people who had the most influence in your childhood. Usually this would be mother and father, though it could be a carer or stepparent. Create a space for each person - so that you have spaces for all the important adults who were in your life when you were a child. For simplicity I will assume you have two spaces - one for mother and one for father, and I will refer to these as (iii) and (iv). You can do these in either order, but I will start with Mother.

4. Write a name, e.g. Mum, on a post-it note and place it somewhere in the room (iii). Describe this person and their characteristics. If you summed her up in five words, what would those words be?

5. From your neutral position (i), what similarities, or very strong differences, are there between your mother (iii) and your partner or the person represented by space (ii)? It is best to use the client's words, e.g. 'between your Mum and Tom'.

6. Look at space (iv), likely to represent your father, and describe this person and their characteristics. If you summed him up in five words, what would those words be?

7. Thinking about your 'Dad' (again use the client's words) in space (iv) from space (i), your neutral perspective, what similarities are there between your Dad (iv) and your partner (ii)?

8. What strikes you about the patterns and characteristics of your partner (ii) and how they relate (or do not relate) to your Mum and Dad (iii and iv)? Note that sometimes we choose a person whose characteristics are the exact opposite of our parents, e.g. if I had a very controlling parent I might have chosen someone who has aspects that are controlling, because it was familiar (even though I might not have liked it as a child) or I might have gone to the other extreme, and chosen someone exceptionally permissive or indulgent. It is interesting to become aware of where you have reacted against a parental style.

9. Having asked questions to check what the client has noticed, the coach can now respectfully, and tentatively, - with great rapport - add in their own observations if they think there is something(s) that the client has not yet noticed.

Exercise 2b - Transforming 'Hot buttons'

1. Sometimes couples develop 'hot buttons'. These are areas of excessive sensitivity. For example, if in your childhood you had a father who shouted and was very angry, it often follows that should your partner raise his voice just a small amount, you may experience him as shouting, even when the volume is only at 5 out of 10. What behaviours does your partner exhibit that push your hot buttons? How might these hot buttons relate to what happened in your key family relationships as a child? Were these characteristics that your parents had?

2. If you have found one or more hot buttons that relate to childhood, put a tiny piece of tissue paper out to represent the 'negative trait' that you see in your partner. Place that paper representing the negative trait (ideally name it as you do it, for example, 'this represents his aggression') on to the

post-it note at space (iii) that represents your partner.

3. There may - or may not - be other areas of excessive sensitivity which are actually attributable to your parents rather than your partner. This is not to say that your partner does not behave in this way at all, but you may have developed a high sensitivity to this behaviour due to the primary wound from your childhood. Make a small piece of paper to represent each class of behaviour or trait and put each one on to the post-it note representing your partner.

4. Take time to reflect. There may be one, or several pieces of tissue on your partner's post-it note, representing behaviours and patterns that were present in your childhood. Take a moment to really recognise and assimilate this information.

5. Now it is time to move those traits back to where they originated. The purpose of this is to 'take the load' off the current experience with your partner, so that when you experience the negative behaviour you simply experience the 'here and now,' and don't also experience the reverberating 'there and then' of your childhood. You may wish to either do this yourself, or ask your coach to do it for you. Decide which fits you best.

6. The process is achieved by moving the pieces of tissue representing the negative trait, from the space representing your partner (ii) and putting them back into the space where they orginiated - (iii or iv), representing the parent with whom you originally experienced the behaviour. With great reverence and ceremony, the small piece of tissue representing the 'negative trait' is plucked off the space representing your partner (by you or your coach) and slowly and deliberately placed back on to the original parent. For example, the negative trait of aggression would be plucked off your partner and slowly, reverently placed back onto Dad (iv). Words may accompany this, such as "This does not belong to Tom (your partner). It was your father that expressed aggressive (or weak, critical etc.) patterns and behaviours."

7. Check what the client notices in their body after this step has been taken.

8. If there are other pieces of tissue representing negative traits then repeat this process, one piece at a time checking with the client what they notice

after each one, until all pieces of tissue are back in the spaces representing parents - the place where they originated.

9. Check how the client feels now and what happens in their body as they look at the space representing their partner who no longer has the negative traits 'sitting' on him or her.

Additional Notes

This last exercise can create a profound shift, so calibrate the appropriate speed for the client of moving the 'negative traits' back. Some clients need a few moments between each one to assimilate, others like to get them all moved quite quickly.

Sometimes I do this exercise with objects rather than post-it notes. I don't let the client use their own objects (e.g. their handbag or mine), as both are 'loaded' with extra significance, but they are invited to pick neutral objects that are in the room. This adds another dimension of size and colour. For example they might pick a red velvet cushion for their father, and an empty plastic cup for their mother. You can ask them what it means to them that they have picked a large cushion for their father and a small plastic cup for their mother. This might add another level of information.

We carry all our experiences with us. As Al Pesso says "Present consciousness is woven of the tapestry of memory." Inevitably our intimate relationships trigger old anchors and unresolved issues. But the brain is extraordinary and this exercise can change our perceptions of our partner very quickly, making it easier to relate to them in more straightforward ways that are not contaminated with the past.

Alpha Leadership

by
Anne Deering

"Only connect."

E M Forster

Biography of Anne Deering

Anne is an executive coach with 30 years business experience in Europe and North America, primarily in the areas of leadership development and change management. She coaches individuals and leadership teams in a variety of corporate and not-for-profit organisations. In 2013 Anne graduated from Meyler Campbell's Business Coach Programme (accredited by the Worldwide Association of Business Coaches). She is a Master Practitioner of NLP and has incorporated a number of NLP models and tools into her work both as a coach and management consultant.

Prior to becoming a coach, Anne was a partner with A.T. Kearney Management Consultants, leading the Organisation and Transformation Practice in Europe. She served on the board of A.T. Kearney and co-authored Alpha Leadership and The Partnering Imperative.

You can contact Anne Deering through Linked In.

Alpha Leadership is a practical framework for understanding how to be an effective business leader – and how to coach business leaders to be the best they can be.

Alpha Leadership grew from working with leaders in a wide range of businesses who were struggling to build organisations that could operate effectively and innovate successfully, while maintaining some sense of personal satisfaction and fulfilment. Many times we heard the comment, "There must be more to life than this" from leaders overwhelmed by the demands of their day to day tasks. Alpha Leadership helps leaders reconnect with their personal mission, building alignment both within themselves and their organisations, so that they can innovate based on anticipating future business imperatives and so that they can create coalitions to act effectively.

Outcomes for the session

This session is aimed at both business leaders and the executive coaches who support them. The session is designed to help participants integrate the Alpha Leadership model into their own practice, providing simple tools and exercises to build leadership capability in practical ways.

Background

Robert Dilts, Julian Russell and I developed the Alpha Leadership model based on a wide range of research and experience. We have each worked with business leaders for decades, from Silicon Valley to rust belt industries; in the United States, Europe and Asia; and in contexts as diverse as traditional management consultancy; the development of NLP and its application in business; dot.com venture 'cataclysm' and funding; and the modelling of leadership behaviour spanning decades of business performance.

As our conclusions took shape, we became increasingly convinced that traditional approaches to leadership place far too much emphasis on action, and not nearly enough emphasis on anticipation and alignment. It is the volatility of the environments and the networked, knowledge-based nature of the organisations in which action has to be taken that make anticipation and alignment so crucial. We observed that leadership skills key to success in today's corporate world are not taught in business schools, are rarely discussed by business academics, nor are they recognised within corporations as they recruit, promote and train their staff.

We noticed that business conversation was all about the 'war for talent' – and yet the solutions presented were all 'outside-in' (what the corporation needed to do to ensure people stayed, to 'make' their values align, to retain them) rather than 'inside-out' (the alignment of an individual's sense of purpose with how he or she spends time at work, and the fit of an individual's skills to the demands of the job).

In developing this model we sought to fill some of these gaps in the lexicon of leadership.

Work-life balance?

It is impossible to write about leadership in the 21st century without making reference to work-life balance. The statistics are daunting: 76% of managers want to spend more time with their families; 50% say they feel too mentally and physically exhausted to do anything but work or sleep; 30% say their lives are out of control; one in five say they are too stressed to enjoy their lives at all.

And yet we have never been more materially successful: we earn more than ever before, we have more purchasing power, more leisure travel, and our children have more material possessions.

So what is going wrong? An extreme imbalance seems to be at work, where success in the workplace spells dismal failure in other parts of our lives. We are all familiar with the symptoms of today's executive malaise – knowing the airport lounge better than your own living room; pushing the 'door close' button on the elevator, because five seconds is too long a wait; children who are happier being comforted after a nightmare by granny, nanny, or the babysitter (just about anyone but you, the parent); the overwhelming sense of overload and the desperate feeling that there is no way out.

There is a way out. We believe that with a new definition of leadership, and with some practical tools and approaches that can be readily applied in our daily lives as leaders, we can take control over our business lives and enjoy living them again. We need a different model of business leadership if company leaders are to learn how to do their job of making things happen without becoming what one senior executive's spouse called 'vice president of long hours and no fun'.

Alpha Leadership is a model designed to help leaders focus in areas where they can have the most impact, for themselves and for their organisations:

- Anticipate - Getting ahead of the curve, detecting weak signals and having the agility of mind and resource to act on them

- Align - Connecting with your core purpose, and from there the ability to form coalitions for change, managing task through relationship

- Act - Focusing on the 80:20; being prepared to act fast; sticking with your goals and adjusting the means as you go.

Each element is made up of three critical skills:

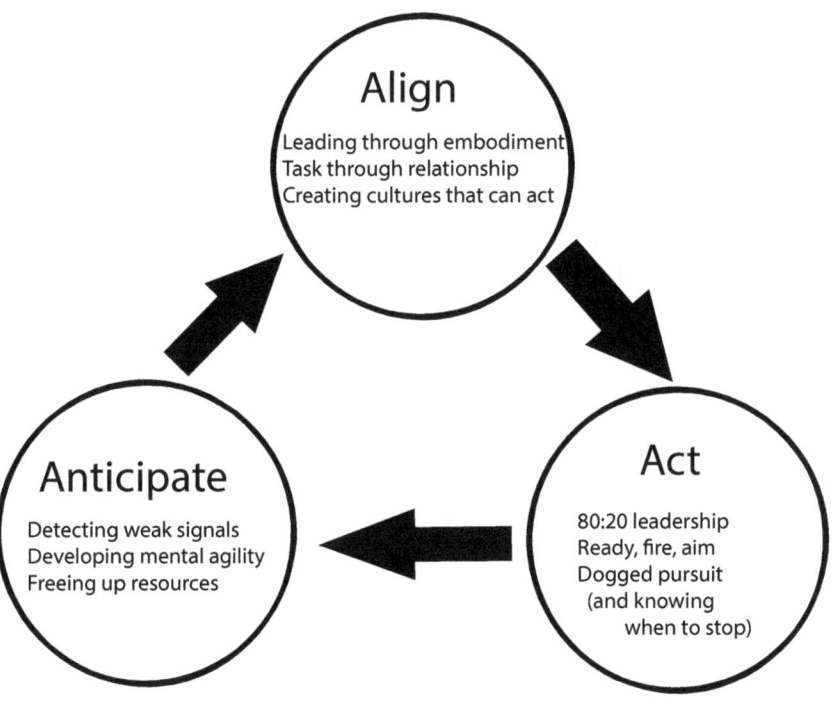

Anticipate

Anticipation starts with detecting weak signals. Everyone can hear a shout, but only those with exceptional sensory systems can hear the barely audible whispers where most of the opportunities and timely warnings lie. Successful leaders create mechanisms within their organisations that allow them to get a step ahead of competition, and have the following characteristics:

- feed real-time information into the organisation

- rely on external, rather than internal, data

- foster dialogue

- generate complete pictures of the market, across all dimensions (supply chain, customers, competitors, employees)

- feed information gathered directly into key decision making processes and incorporate follow-through action

- all of the above are repeated rhythmically and over short cycles

When weak signals are detected, only those organisations with highly developed mental agility will be able to incorporate these new insights into their strategies. Key to this agility is the concept of 'fixed purpose, responsive goals, variable means' – a strongly held core purpose that is open to changing external scenarios and shifting implementation plans. Organisational diversity is a key component in building the mental agility of leaders. The ability to build multiple interpretations, or 'maps', of any given circumstance will strongly influence the organisation's responsiveness.

Those who detect weak signals and incorporate them into their strategic plans must also be able to free up resources to exploit these early insights. Options are worthless if they are not exercised. Organisations that lack the necessary flexibility to redeploy assets quickly, and whose leaders are not always on the lookout for more profitable deployments of those assets, will be vanquished by more agile organisations led by more alert executives. Highly agile organisations find ways to allow resources to 'flock' to those parts of the business with most chances of success.

Align

Leading through embodiment starts with the alignment of what you value and how you spend your life, whether at work or at home. Personal alignment is probably the single most effective remedy for stress and dissatisfaction in the workplace and beyond. A high level of personal alignment gives you the charisma, congruence, and vision that will inspire the people in your care to act effectively. Powerful leaders are fully aligned in every element of what Robert Dilts has called Neuro-Logical Levels:

- What I am a part of – context, self-transcendence, spirit

- Who I am – identity

- What I believe – beliefs, values, motivations

- What I am capable of – skills, competences, ambition

- What I do – behaviour, actions

- Where I do it – external surroundings

Unfortunately it is easy to get out of alignment on any one of these levels and as a result to experience stress, anxiety, and a feeling that what we are doing lacks meaning. We can ignore these incongruities, often for many years, but they will eventually take their toll on our motivation, our energy, and even our health.

Effective leaders focus on task through relationship. At a team level, leaders focus on aligning the relationships and coalitions of people that get the job done, rather than just concentrating on the task itself. Paradoxically, the powerful leader's key tool in getting people to follow is first to understand what other people want and where they want to go. As a leader, your skills in team alignment will help get things done and avoid the frustrations of missed deadlines and inaction. A wide range of NLP models are useful in this context, particularly using matching strategies to pace and lead, focusing on positive intentions and using perceptual positions to build strong stakeholder relationships and coalitions.

Beyond immediate coalitions for change, effective leaders develop and nurture cultures that can act, that is, organisations that are aligned and enabled to act around agreed goals. Cultures that can act have three distinctive qualities:

- They are clear, but adaptable.

- They not only tolerate dissent, they encourage it, because they see it as both a source of novelty and an antidote to the inappropriate and out-dated assumptions and mental models that tend to accumulate within, and constrain, less open cultures.

- They are always on the look-out for feed-back mechanisms that enhance their adaptability and responsiveness and maintain their openness.

Such cultures are rare because it's hard to maintain cultural strength and clarity while indulging mavericks and subversives. It is worth noting that catalytic mechanisms such as those described above and in Exercise 1 are very useful when developing such cultures, because they make flexibility an integral part of the culture rather than a separate quality that a leader has to maintain deliberately.

Act

Prioritising tasks and focusing on where we can add most value is the first step towards eliminating the feelings of stress and overload many of us are experiencing. Have you ever had a sinking feeling when you log on to discover 80 emails demanding your attention? Do you dread going on vacation because of the work backlog that will be waiting for you on your return? Do you finish the day wondering how you can have been so frenetically busy achieving so little? 80:20 leadership builds awareness of where you add most value as a leader and enhances your ability to focus on those tasks where you are the 'difference that makes the difference'.

Many attempts to change organisations get bogged down in the early stages of implementation often due to the sheer complexity and scale of the change required. A key leadership skill is the ability to create safe experiments that allow change to be proved while using timely 'in-course correction' to secure future results – in other words, Ready, Fire, Aim. This approach can reduce frustration and wasted effort by breaking through log-jams, particularly where these are caused by the organisation's reluctance to act until a perfect solution has been found.

There is a subtle difference between persistence and stubbornness and it is vitally important to know the difference. Dogged Pursuit is a key skillset – not blindly persisting in actions that have failed to deliver results but having the determination, drive, resilience and sheer imagination to pursue outcomes and overcome obstacles to implementation. High performance organisations stick at things. Their leaders display dogged pursuit in the attainment of core goals, maintaining perseverance and constancy of purpose over long periods of time.

This energy and commitment has ripple effects throughout the organisation, converting 'faddishness' into a long-term dedication to the achievement of strongly held goals. Dogged pursuit also requires leaders to acknowledge where particular routes to a goal are blocked, and where certain initiatives could be more profitably directed. In other words, they pay attention to where the organisation should stop, rather than focusing exclusively on where it should start afresh.

Exercises and Activities

Exercise 1 - Detecting Weak Signals

Outcomes:

(For business leaders) Improve your organisation's weak signal detection by strengthening existing processes

(For business coaches) Learn how to help coaching clients improve their organisation's weak signal detection by strengthening existing processes

Working in pairs, allow 40 minutes (2 x 20 minute slots) for this exercise

Instructions:

Partner 1: Choose a process that is currently used in your or your coaching client's organisation to elicit information from the market. Typical examples of these types of processes include customer quality feedback; market research; competitor analysis.

Assess the process you have chosen against the checklist of effective weak signal detection mechanisms (see Exercise 1 handout).

How many of these characteristics are present in the process you are assessing? What two actions could you or your client take to fill gaps you have identified? What would be a first step towards taking these actions?

Partner 2: Coach your partner through this process by probing for gaps and eliciting actions and first steps. Then swap and repeat.

Exercise 1 handout: Detecting Weak Signals

	Present in current process?	Action to fill gap?	First step?
Feeds real time information into the business			
Relies on external, rather than internal, data			
Fosters dialogue			
Generates complete pictures of the market, across all dimensions (supply chain, customers, competitors, employees)			
Feeds information gathered directly into key decision making processes and incorporates follow-through action			
Is repeated rhythmically and over short cycles			

Exercise 2 - Leading Through Embodiment

Outcomes:

(For business leaders) Identify ways to enhance your personal alignment and satisfaction

(For business coaches) Become familiar with a tool to help coaching clients enhance their personal alignment and satisfaction

Working in pairs, allow 60 minutes (2 x 30 minute slots) for this exercise.

Instructions:

Partner 1: Review the prompt questions in the handout against each of the six Neuro-Logical levels. Focus on one or two levels where you feel there are particular opportunities to increase your sense of alignment or where you are experiencing some incongruence that you would like to address. Summarise the strengths that support your leadership ability. Summarise the development areas that may undermine your leadership ability.

Working with your partner, talk through what you can do to increase your strengths and reduce your weaknesses. Look for any ways in which the levels are not aligned with each other: for example, does your behaviour align with your values? Are there still gaps which affect the congruence of either your behaviour or your sense of identity? Is your environment congruent with your values? Identify steps to improve alignment.

Partner 2: Coach your partner through this process, eliciting actions and first steps. Then swap and repeat.

Exercise 2 handout: Leading Through Embodiment

	Strengths	Development areas	What can I do about it?
Environment	What are the good things about my environment? What works for me? What works for other people?	What are the unpleasant things? What doesn't work for me? What doesn't work for other people?	
Behaviour	What do I do that works? That achieves my objectives?	What do I do that doesn't work? That doesn't achieve my objectives?	
Capabilities	What are my strong skills?	Which skills do I lack?	
Beliefs and values	What values do I have that support who I am and where I am going? What beliefs do I have that make me stronger?	What values do I have that interfere with who I am and where I am going? What beliefs undermine me?	
Identity	What are the helpful things about my sense of identity?	What are the things about who I am that I feel undermine me? How can I turn these elements of my identity to my advantage?	
Spiritual	What are the benefits of my sense of meaning in life?	What are the disadvantages of my sense of meaning in life?	

Exercise 3 - 80/20 Leadership - Value Planning

The following tool will help you determine the amount of time you allocate to the portfolio of activities that convert your values into practice.

The outcomes are:

(For business leaders) Increase your impact by focusing on those activities and collaborations that add most value to your business

(For business coaches) Become familiar with a tool to help coaching clients increase their impact by focusing on those activities and collaborations that add most value to their business

Working in pairs, allow 60 mins (2 x 30 min slots) for this exercise.

Instructions:

Partner 1: List the mix of your activities that deliver most value to your organisation. Use the time allocation worksheet in handout 3 to note these activities. Write the list of activities in the spaces in the middle of the worksheet. On the pie chart on the right, under the column Desired State, represent the percentage of time you will need to allocate to each activity if the values are to be successfully established.

Now review what you have specified as the allocation you would like, and compare it to the time you actually spend on these activities. Using the pie charts on the left hand side of the worksheet, represent the relative amounts of time you are currently spending with respect to each activity. Use rough estimates at this stage – although you may want to go back through your diary after the workshop and work out in an average month how much actual time you spend on these priority activities. You may be surprised!

Do the same with the second half of the worksheet. List the people or groups of people with whom you are collaborating in order to undertake these activities. Note the proportion of your time you would like to spend with them in order to be successful in your priority activities, and note this on the right side of the worksheet. Compare these percentages with the time you actually spend with each individual or group, noted on the left side of the worksheet.

Remember, optimally you would be investing the majority of your time in the people and activities that produce 80% of your value to your organisation. What activities would you reduce or cut out? Which would you increase? With whom would you need to spend more time or less time? And what do you need to do to make this happen?

Partner 2: Coach your partner through this process, helping them make a rough estimate of how much time they spend on priority activities and with their most important stakeholders.

Elicit what actions they might take to rebalance the present state more towards their desired state in terms of time spent, particularly emphasising what they would need to stop doing in order to make this a reality. Then swap and repeat.

Exercise 3 - 80/20 Leadership - Value Planning

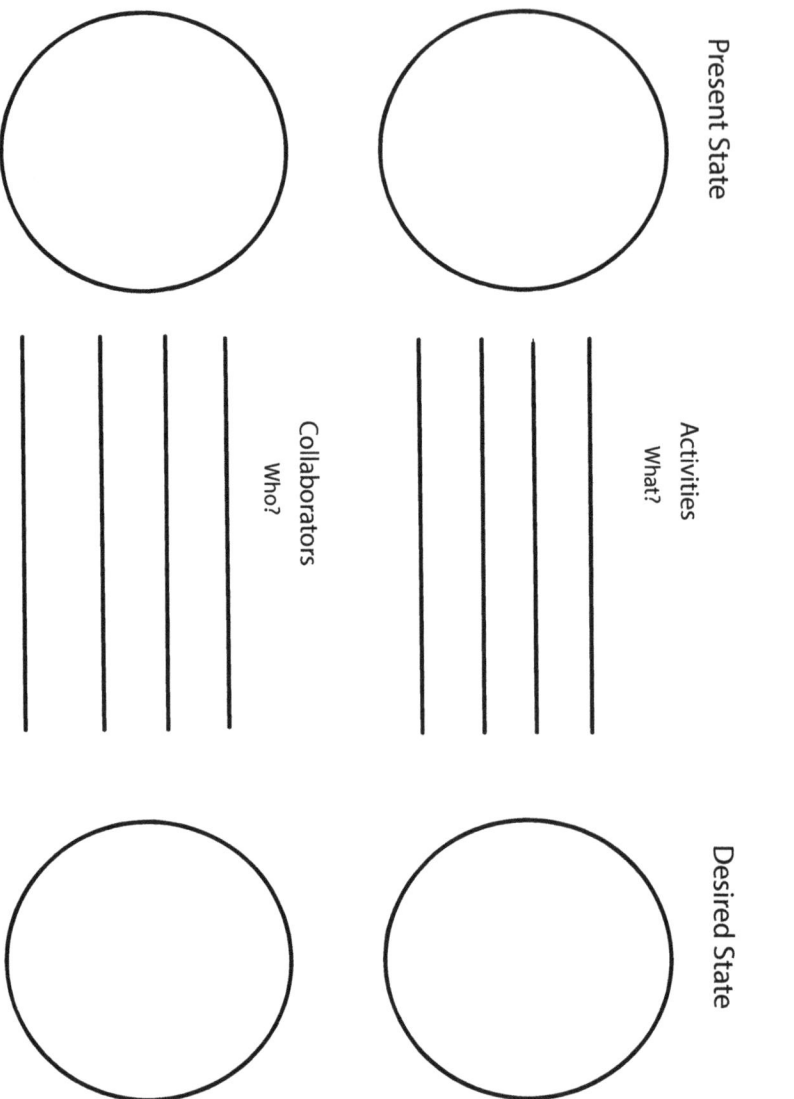

Present State

Value Planning: Time Allocation Worksheet

Collaborators
Who?

Activities
What?

Desired State

EXPLORING
OTHER WORLDS

by
Dido Fisher

"I believe that intuition is a 'muscle' that can be strengthened."

Biography of Dido Fisher

Dido is an accomplished trainer, facilitator and coach with 20 years experience of training across a variety of industries for high profile companies and organisations and has presented at conferences around the world. She is presently facilitating programmes around non-verbal communication skills for medical students and healthcare professionals at Kings, Barts and St Thomas's hospitals in London. As well as organisations she works prolifically with individuals particularly around areas of confidence, health, creativity and special needs. She is a certified NLP Trainer and incorporates NLP thinking and techniques into all aspects of her work. For the same length of time she has practised NLP, she has also been an Equine Behaviourist and has been integrating these two practices for almost two decades.

Her trainings are often described as engaging, meaningful and fun. Dido has a passion for finding what makes learning valuable to a particular individual or group. She likes to cross-pollinate and share best practice across genres of industry, in order to support people's accessibility and success in the ideas and visions that beckon them.

www.intuitive-leadership.co.uk

I focus on training the skills of self-leadership. I'm interested in increasing people's individual capacity and power that can then be applied in any given field, both professionally and personally. I work with all kinds of people from business leaders, artists, people with special-needs, to adults and children on a Hero's Journey. The beauty of this practice group session is that it can be adapted for the needs and benefits of any diverse group.

This practice group involves experiential work and an exploration through some of the fields of NLP learning we revel in; observation, calibration, rapport, positional flexibility, intent and energy.

What would the fish say if it could fly, and the bird if it could swim? What riches will be revealed for you when you reach outside your own world and traverse a map of truly different meta programmes? These riches often hold a uniqueness uncommon to that found in our routines. Which is why I choose to work with horses at Intuitive Leadership, who I believe are the Somatic Kings, and the most elegant and honest reflectors of personal change. What would the human say if you could harness the power and sensory agility of the horse and dip a toe into the world of equus? What will you learn by exploring other worlds with us?

Background

When coaching and teaching clients or teams that appear 'difficult', it can often be because the bond of rapport and paced communication has been lost. At times Coaches and Trainers confuse a true 2nd position (see Perceptual Positions Model in appendix) of an individual with mind reading or content directing. Indeed, sometimes because Coaches and Leaders have more training and increased informational skills, there can be a greater self-belief in their interpretation of a client as being correct because the training suggests so, rather than taking training principles as the frame, and each individual as just that, an individual.

I have created these exercises to move people right out of the cognitive and observational position and into the somatic self where true 2nd position reading can provide a balancing container for skills and knowledge. From this integrated centre, intuition can begin to flourish. I believe that intuition is a muscle that can be strengthened when attention and intention is directed appropriately on self and other.

This is also an excellent exercise for 'Training the Trainer' events, as it allows feedback on skills to be given in a non-verbal, compassionate but very clear vehicle whilst bypassing people's language barriers.

A 'difficult' horse or a horse with a difficult problem?

In this chapter you will see me working with a horse called Dillon. Dillon came to me as a rescue horse, still wild and untamed, he couldn't be touched and was terrified of people. It was two years before he stopped hiding at the back of his stable when there was someone on the stable yard. Due to a change in circumstances his previous human repeatedly asked me to take him on despite my physical incapacity - due to a spinal injury, I had at the time lost the full use of my right arm and was incredibly vulnerable to any kind of physical pressure.

Dillon was trained loose, free and able to express himself as he chose. He was never tied or restrained. To do so would have been what he was anticipating based on his brief previous experiences with humans and ropes. It would have also been catastrophic in relation to my recovery at the time. Dillon was not trained to respond to food rewards, but instead to sourcing comfort within our physical movements. He was not a 'difficult' horse but one carrying a story he needed to 'discuss', which was a fundamental problem he had with people that he needed to resolve.

My intention was to guide his terror into attention, attention into awareness, and his awareness into curiosity. It took 1000 repetitions. In each repetition his challenge was: "Can you still believe in me now?" In every response my answer had to come from a space held for him which just said "yes" despite the size of the step he took forward or backwards. Dillon remains one of the most sensitive animals I have worked with. I never wanted to take his sensitivities away from him, but to support him to use his sensitivities in ways that don't scare him and give very articulate feedback.

Although this chapter shows pictures of me with Dillon, in this practice group participants will each be invited to step into the perceptual position and experience of a horse and be trained by a 'horse trainer'. This is using the 'as if' imaginative play frame to access a non-human 2nd Position. I offer below more information about the subjective experience of horses and suggestions for how people may achieve this sensitive, equine 2nd position as closely as they can.

In instructions for exercises 2 and 3 the visual demonstrations referred to are facilitated demonstrations of the exercises in which the group facilitator is the trainer and someone from the group plays the horse. During this demonstration the rest of the group are in the observer role and there are instructions, question and suggestions for this.

Outcomes for the session

This session is designed to:

- Deepen NLP skills into the muscle

- Re-attune sensory acuity to self and others

- Learn to shape and anchor your own behaviour elegantly

- Enhance communication by flowing naturally through the perceptual positions

- Elicit the implicit contracts in communication and create new discernment in engagement

- Learn more about states of congruence, presence and alignment and how to access them more immediately

- Experience and experiment with alternative meta programmes, allowing the inclusion of new updated versions of the self

- Notice more, but by doing less, and gain more energy

- Increase leading and coaching capabilities

- Become increasingly intuitive

Menu of key tools, models and skills

- Rapport

- Calibration

- State management

- Anchoring

- Pacing and leading

- Nested T.O.T.E's

- Sensory acuity

- Modeling behaviour implicitly

- Shaping behaviour, both self and other

- Chunking with flexibility to appropriate levels of change

- Perceptual positions shifts through 1st, 2nd, 3rd, and 4th

- Representational systems observation – physiology

- Chain of excellence

- Leadership styles elicitation

- Critical submodalities, tracking the trigger, the difference that makes a difference

- Embodiment of the basic Presuppositions of NLP in a living movement form

Exercises and Activities

Exercise 1 – Centring

With the whole group; 5 minutes

Outcome - to bring individuals into their centre, quieten the cognitive mind and increase their kinaesthetic calibrating senses.

Instructions to the group:

1. Stand up and notice your breathing.

2. Close your eyes if possible and safe. Feel free to open your eyes to check in with where you are at any point if you need to, and then close them again

when you're ready.

3. Now notice the balance of weight of your body by rolling on your feet. Are you tending to lean forward, backwards or sideways?

4. Slightly relax, or unlock, your knees.

5. By rolling very slowly from your heels to the balls and toes of your feet, find the 'balance neutral' point, where the whole of your foot is in contact with the floor and your weight is balanced over the middle of your foot.

6. Next, roll your hips forwards, backwards and side to side gently; again find balance neutral, the point that your balanced hips are most balanced over your feet.

7. Now roll your shoulders forwards, backwards and side to side gently; again find balance neutral, the point that your balanced shoulders are most balanced over your balanced hips over your balanced feet.

8. Now very gently - do not roll, but move - your head from side to side and back and forth; find the most balanced place for your head over your balanced shoulders, over your balanced hips, over your balanced feet.

9. Next, imagine the air and space above you aligning to your found sense of balance and then adjusting to fit you perfectly. Notice the air and space down your arms and legs, and front and back, making space and support for this found sense of balance.

10. Now in this state of found balance, imagine breathing your breath into every part of your body, every corner and nuance and say to yourself: "I am here, I am present, I am awake." Those of you who have not already done so, please open your eyes.

Exercise 2 – Training your Horse and Letting your Horse Train You

In pairs; allow 45 minutes

> 5 minutes visual demonstration
> 10 minutes A is the horse, B is the trainer,
> Then reverse roles for another 10 minutes
> 10 minutes shared feedback between horses and trainers
> 10 minutes shared group feedback from all pairs

Outcomes

- deepening embodiment of NLP skills; state management, calibration, pacing and leading, anchoring and shaping

- facilitating change from our centre through implicit modelling

- creating a space for honest feedback

Demonstration and Observation hints

Whilst watching the demonstration of the horse and trainer, use your observation and calibration skills to notice and consider some of these questions:

- from position 1 - the horse

- position 2 - the trainer

- position 3 - the observer

1. Who is pacing and who is leading?

2. What and who are shaping behaviour?

3. How do you know rapport is changing?

4. What is most prominent about each of those involved?

5. Does this change, and if so when? What creates that change?

6. What are you aware of in your own body throughout the exercise?

7. What does the whole look like/feel like when things are going well?

Directions for A - the horse

- Horse you are a highly sensitive and reactive creature.

- You are generally 'away from' (NLP meta programme).

- You live in peripheral vision and you see and notice everything.

- You don't like being stared at; you feel safe when eyes are averted from you.

- Sharp movements spook you; soft movements calm you.

- You are guided by kinaesthetic information. Things need to feel right and safe for you: when they do you are ready to stay calmer and more still; when they aren't you want to move away until things feel safer.

- When your trainer steps away from you, notice what you notice about how you feel. Trust your responses! You may only be playing at being a horse, but intuitive leadership skills cross all species and if you respond as you feel you will be giving the most honest feedback.

- You have total freedom to express your honest response to your trainer's actions.

- However, please do not be violent with teeth or hooves! They are only learning to be good trainers.

- Please be honest when you notice a shift. Try to be neither difficult nor helpful, just honest. It's the best help you can be.

Directions for B - the trainer

Your nested outcomes and T.O.T.E. are as follows;

>   to get your horse to stand still

>   to get your horse to stand while being stroked on the shoulder

>   to get your horse to follow you

- Your horse is wild - only go as far as you calibrate is optimum for your horse.

- You are a human; humans have foveal vision. If you look directly at your horse she or he may be spooked. Use your peripheral vision when attempting to get close to your horse.

- Showing the front of your body to your horse will drive him or her away; showing your side or back will encourage him or her to follow.

- Remember, unless you pace and lead your horse with intuitive calibration and create rapport he or she will run away.

Directions

1. Both A and B stand facing in the same direction, shoulder to shoulder. A then can choose how far away to stand from B, between 5-10 feet as a starting point.

2. Staying in peripheral vision, B begins to step sideways towards A.

3. A must react as he or she sees fit. A may step sideways, away or toward, or move forwards or backwards and at any speed he or she chooses.

4. B's job is to 'mirror' A by stepping back, or towards or away, as A does.

5. B, if your horse runs away forwards or backwards your job is to follow and mirror that movement *until* he or she stops. When he or she stops then step away as quickly as you can.

6. Step away from the horse for a few moments then begin the process again. Step back towards the horse and mirror her or his actions. Again, when she or he stops moving step away as swiftly as you can.

7. Repeat this process until your horse understands that if she runs you follow and if she stops you step away.

8. Each time, you're looking to be a little closer when the horse stops, and for her or him to stop a little sooner.

9. If you calibrate the horse correctly, pace and lead, this will move in this positive direction.

10. If you notice your horse is becoming wilder with you rather than tamer, what do you notice about your own state, breathing, beliefs and intentions of behaviour? What could you calm to make you feel safer to your horse?

Feedback Questions

- What did you notice working when your horse reacted positively?

- What behaviours didn't work as a trainer?

- What adjustments did you need to make to bring things back on track when they weren't working so well?

- As a horse, how did you feel towards your trainer?

- What were your beliefs about your horse when you were the trainer?

- What was the sense of relationship between you? What did you do to incubate that sense of relationship?

- What was your role in facilitating a sense of safety as the trainer?

- What skills can you take into enhancing your coaching or leadership work?

Exercise 3 – Dissolving fear with silent sponsorship

In pairs, allow 30 minutes for this exercise.

5 minutes visual demonstration

15 minutes both A and B sponsor and be sponsored

5 minutes shared feedback between pairs

5 minutes shared group feedback from all pairs

Beyond the common definition of commercial sponsorship lies a notion that we can 'sponsor' a person's new choices and actions either by an action of support of our own, or by simply 'holding space'. Holding space is an action of sponsorship which offers another the gift of belief in their choices, in their ability to learn something new, and the possibility of a new outcome for them. This act of support without advice or direction as to what that person 'should' do not only supports growth in a specific area, but also engages a deeper meta message about an individual's ability to make good choices.

I always use this resource when working with horses. It's the first foundation, without which training can appear like dominance. When coaching, congruent sponsorship alone can be all that is needed for a person to step across a tipping point threshold in their world.

Outcomes

- Translating learnings from earlier embodiment exercises into participants' practical daily lives. An exercise to calibrate and notice the effects we can have in support, sponsorship, coaching and leadership without words.

- Creating a foundation from which words can be added back in the 'speaking world' with greater congruence, power and effect.

Directions

Choose who will be A (sponsored) and who will be B (sponsor) first, and in the time frame make sure both get to experience both roles.

1. A chooses a low to medium level challenge, labels it appropriately and places the label (a word or symbol) on a piece of A4 paper.

2. B invites A to position this paper representing the challenge somewhere between 5 to 10 feet at a distance that feels 'right'.

3. B anchors a positive state in A in the space A is - at selected distance from the challenge. This is the space A will come back to later.

4. B supports and sponsors A to step closer and closer to their challenge represented on paper through *silent* sponsorship. This encouragement can be done from the front, from behind or alongside. It may be highly active or quietly present. It may stay uniform throughout or it may change as the journey progresses. It will not involve touch.

5. The purpose of this journey is for B to calibrate the most effective form of support for A.

6. The purpose of this journey for A is to notice the difference it makes to be sponsored and supported when contemplating the challenge.

7. Once A has reached the space representing their challenge, B will ask A to notice what they see hear and feel now whilst being supported to stand in their challenge position. What can they take back to their original state which will make the challenge state easier to deal with in the future?

8. Once stated, B establishes a kinaesthetic anchor on A's arm and asks A to walk back to their original space, taking the updated information with them.

9. From the original space, looking back at the challenge with their updated information, B asks A what he or she notices is different.

Further comments

This practice group session is based on experiential somatic explorative exercises. Although it's possible to work with the exercises in smaller spaces, the more space available to experiment the better. Move chairs and tables out of the way, access corridors and open spaces, or if at all possible use the outdoors.

Some of these exercises naturally encourage a degree of fun and playfulness though there are powerful lessons and skills to take away from the processes. Encouraging and framing the fun elements are essential for me as this:

- encourages individuals to overcome any self-consciousness about playing a horse

- invites individuals to engage freely with the process so finding their individual, authentic learnings

- provides the oxygen from movement and endorphins from laughter which create great neuro-nutrition for new learning pathways and behaviours.

Zen in The Art of The NLP Meta Model

by

Judith Lowe

*"The world of Zen
is the world of
pure experience
without concepts."*

THICHT NHAT HAHN

Biography of Judith Lowe

Judith Lowe is one of the most experienced, committed, effective and engaging teachers in NLP. Judith has worked for many years with clients from a diverse range of professional backgrounds in the public and private sectors, both in-house and on public programmes, at every level of NLP, providing innovative, in-depth, skills-based NLP training and coaching.

She is known for her warmth, wit and wide reading, as well as her overall dedication to giving her students and clients the very best of advanced, systemic NLP. She is on the board of the Association for NLP (ANLP) and a founder member of the Professional Guild of NLP.

www.judithlowe.com

'Zen is the Un-Symbolisation of the World.'

This chapter is about a way of practising and coaching with the NLP Meta Model with a skilful, soft, relational and open coaching style. The Meta Model tends to be introduced on a Practitioner programme as an information-gathering tool and then is used in a somewhat linear, quick-fire, interrogatory mode.

Here the process is deliberately slowed down and the coach encourages the client to bring a gentle awareness, sense of spaciousness, relaxation and curiosity to the process. The client then explores and transforms their issue or situation, in relation to more of a felt sense of the infinite possible forms and meanings available. This can often be a profoundly creative and self-renewing process.

I have presented variations of this session at NLP practice groups, the NLP Conference and Masterclass days as well as on PPD Learning Practitioner and Master Practitioner programmes.

The NLP Meta Model of Language – What is it?

The NLP Meta Model is one of the core models in NLP. It's a model about how the way that we use language can create certain kinds of traps, flaws and limitations in our thinking.

The challenges to these patterns in natural, spoken language are offered, in the Meta Model, through a set of questions specifically designed to 'force' changes, new frames and useful clarifications in the client's perceived reality.

The questions constitute an artful and practical coach's toolset. They stimulate and reveal new potential meanings, causes, categories, judgements, projections, comparisons and information that can expand and enrich the client's 'map' and world. This allows the client spontaneously to perceive and create new, quality goals and choices in their issue or situation.

Background notes

The NLP Meta-Model was originally presented in 'The Structure of Magic', the first NLP book by John Grinder and Richard Bandler. It's a practical handbook for therapists on how to work more effectively with clients who want to change their stuck or painful 'map' of a situation. What makes it unique is that Bandler and Grinder use models, insights and approaches from the academic field of linguistics.

The inspiration and many of the patterns were drawn from their personal observations and modelling of the 'magic' of outstanding therapists Fritz Perls and Virginia Satir. These patterns were subjected to extensive real-world testing and trialling with students and colleagues at the University at Santa Cruz CA. They were eventually expanded and edited to create an elegant and workable model for multiple communication contexts.

The Meta Model is based on the idea that 'the map is not the territory' one of the key guiding principles in NLP. What this means is that our nervous systems and cognitive minds are designed to delete, generalise and distort the mass of information and data our senses process. Without being consciously aware of it we have many kinds of filters and transforms on our experience. What we personally think and feel to be absolutely true and real is largely a subjective, culturally specific kind of simulation of reality.

This personal 'simulation' tends to be more or less good enough to get by in most situations in life. Fortunately, it usually has a reasonable relationship to other people's perceptions, communication, and the so-called 'facts' on the ground.

Language plays a key role in this filtering and modelling of experience. Language doesn't just describe, it actively models and constructs our reality. The NLP Meta Model is a model *about* this modelling process of language.

Sometimes our own language habits create difficulties for us. The words and sentences we select unconsciously can construct unhelpful beliefs, biases and impoverished 'maps' of a situation. The way that we talk about something becomes it's own reality. We can, through our own words and sentences, psychologically constrict ourselves in an unhappy, seemingly unchangeable world. For example, a key feature of anxiety and depression is negative, critical self-talk. Beliefs like "I'm a failure and an idiot", "No-one will ever love me", "I'll never be successful", can be repeated in an inner voice of despair and self-hatred. This process generates it's own reality as the speaker filters their experiences for confirming evidence in a negative spiral of limiting, self-fulfilling beliefs.

Even in relatively non-pathological everyday life, ordinary structures in language make it easy for us to self-deceive and to function from impoverished versions of events. Our inbuilt cognitive biases lead us unknowingly to make errors in judgement and behaviour, some of which are harmful or deluded and entail negative consequences.

The Meta Model is an essential tool for effective communication and coaching. It can help people in many personal and professional situations clarify, communicate and think more effectively, especially in situations of confusion or conflict. And it can help people to expand and enrich their world and their lives in many surprising, delightful and generative ways.

Zen...

"We are looking for a way to feel more real, but we do not realise that to feel more real we have to push ourselves further into the unknown."

Mark Epstein

So why 'Zen' in the art of the Meta Model?

Zen is about living and being. It's a state of mind and a relationship to ourselves, others and the world that is hard to describe.

The sages and saints of Zen tend to paint, write poems and offer riddles to try and describe this special open, aware state and to explain the beauty of life, the natural, living world and the mystery of being.

"The world of Zen is the world of pure experience without concepts."

Thicht Nhat Hahn

... and NLP

There are two related aspects to these Zen-type qualities we can generate in our coaching with the NLP Meta Model. The first of these is the whole mind-body state of the coach and client - as centred, present and awake.

The second aspect concerns the Meta Model questions and the kind of existential enquiry into a person's current 'map' and worldview.

The Zen-like state

In NLP there is a privileged, skilful state sometimes called the 'know–nothing' state. It is related to an optimum state for implicit, unconscious modelling and also to practices like mindfulness, yoga and martial arts in which being centred and present is key. The purpose of this aware and awakened state is to have such clear sensory channels that you have the choice to be fully open to experience, to learning, feedback and personal connection in the living moment.

It's not only an essential state for basic rapport and calibration but also a foundation for generative coaching, personal expression and artistry.

In terms of the visual, auditory, kinaesthetic (VAK) senses, this state is generally characterised by:

V. soft, externally-focused eyes, peripheral and mobile vision, a sense of visual spaciousness - not tight or fixed gaze or primary focus on internal images

A. soft, externally-focused, more panoramic hearing, quiet inside - not inner self-talk

K. soft, awake, aligned, centred, regular deeper breathing, 'sprung' balanced body, often symmetrical graceful movement, gestures, expressions – not excess muscular tension or collapsed relaxation, no fixed asymmetries, no held or irregular breathing

Developing your personal expressions of this aligned, present state is something of a lifelong adventure.

The techniques and questions in NLP, on their own, don't create the changes and new choices. It's the living relationship with the skilful, sensing presence, attunement, attention, mental agility, non-verbal expressiveness and emotional intelligence of the coach that helps the client to create the 'magic'.

The Zen-like enquiry

One of the core questions in the Meta Model is the epistemological question 'How do you know?' It is used to challenge the fixed meanings, the cause-effect structures of logic, the value judgements, the habitual categorisation and meaning-attribution of experience, the comparisons and the potentially distorted perceptions of other people's internal experience and much more.

An apparently simple question, it profoundly challenges many of the ways in which we hold our 'maps' together to construct our partial, apparently coherent pasts and presents and our limited, predictable futures.

Do we really know? Are we sure? Are these verifiable facts? What are the evidences? How robust and sensory-based are they? The questions trigger a focused search and allow a client to perceive freshly where the data is weak, ambiguous or missing.

Sometimes this search can take someone beyond their ordinary habituated filters to a genuine 'not-knowing', and to an experience of an unknown and un-patterned 'map' in which new perceptions and choices can be sensed.

This search bears some relationship to the possible responses to Zen koans, the riddles and puzzles designed to awaken the heart-mind and provoke enlightenment.

Another core question is *"How (specifically) are you X ing?"* where X is a verb and process. The question requests information about the detail and richness of a living process, of change and influence - about actions, relationships, strategies, values and choices. Indeed, at another level, it's the 'how-to' modelling approach of the NLP field that is focused on creating practical, transferable models of genius and outstanding performance.

The Meta Model reconnects us to the embodied, sensory world when we have got lost in the abstract, spin of language. Paradoxically it can also put us more in touch with a kind of spaciousness, emptiness and resourcefulness in the beauty of the present moment. In this mind-body, generative state many new and profoundly meaningful revelations concerning a problem situation can spontaneously emerge.

These types of question can help us experience that we are always in transition and flow. As Heraclitus says "You can't step into the same river twice." Maybe every noun, as Steve Jobs said, really can be verbed.

Crisp autumn leaves
Rustle softly
Then blow away

Outcomes

To help you develop more choice in your skills and style, rather than the somewhat formulaic, interrogative, instrumental way that the Meta Model is sometimes presented.

To reveal more of the inner workings of the patterns, how they work together in a system of logic, and how the coach's Meta Model questions can create positive transformations in the client's 'map'.

The exercises and activities for this chapter are not intended to substitute for a thorough introduction, understanding and practice of all the Meta Model patterns in a classroom context with a skilled teacher.

Exercises

These exercises are best done in groups of three. Allow 20 minutes each way, so an hour in total for the group. The introduction to these exercises is a two-step process as follows:

1. **Meta Model Review** If you are using this chapter as a framework for your NLP practice group then it may be useful briefly to present the patterns in the Meta Model as a 'refresh and review' process first. You can design this to fit your group's learning needs in relation to the overall intention to explore the Meta Model patterns in this more Zen-like mode.

2. **Soft, open Coaching State** The soft, open, awake, relational coaching state can be created in many ways and all of them begin with body awareness:

*   tuning into your breathing and allowing it to deepen and slow down

*   tuning into the way you are sitting, the contact with the chair and the floor

- allowing the spine to lengthen, the back to broaden, the shoulders to widen, drop and soften, your body simultaneously rising up against gravity to the sky and pulled back down by gravity to earth - 'sprung'

- a general body scan, noticing tension, letting it go

- relax the jaw, soften the eyes and look outwards

- slowing down, taking in your surroundings and the infinite space around you and within you, having the feeling of 'all the time in the world'

- enjoying your breathing, tuning and turning to others, soft smiles and acknowledgement

- quietening down, settling in, centring, breathing, coming present

- people who practise meditation, mindfulness, yoga, tai chi, Alexander technique etc. will have reference experiences for this

This state preparation will be the foundation of the coach's, client's and observer's state. The observer or guardian in the exercise can support the coach and the client to maintain the state. Slowing down, pausing and breathing allows everyone to 'not know' and to create space for something new to happen.

I have picked two of the Meta Model patterns for this chapter to give you a flavour of the process. You can choose these or some of the others for your own practice group session.

Work in groups of three: coach, client, observer.

The focus is on the state and the process, rather than on any single kind of result.

Remember not to get caught up in the issue or in feeling. It's not up to you as the coach to solve it. In NLP we say that people have all the resources they need. The coach's role is to help the client explore and transform their 'map' and to help them reconnect to their personal, inner resources in useful, meaningful ways. There is a discipline as well as an art involved in working with the Meta Model. Stay with the state, the relationship, the pattern and the process.

Meta Model Patterns

A. Nominalisations – the Meta Model pattern that helps you turn abstract nouns back into their original verb or process form.

Relationship transforms to relating.

Management to managing.

As the noun transforms back into a verb the speaker re-connects to a living, moving, embodied process again rather than to an abstract thing or object. New experiences, distinctions and choices become more felt, visible and possible and a sense of personal agency and resourcefulness is restored.

When I am introducing this tool in a business training I invite the group to generate a list of examples from their own organisational meetings and documents. This is often quite an entertaining process as the latest buzzwords and apparently empty management slogans are identified and explored. Sometimes the results are surprisingly meaningful and motivational. Often though the process reveals the organisational need for more detailed, sensory-based communication for their visions, strategies, partnership, mission statements, values etc.

Technically speaking, in a Zen-like universe, any noun can be a nominalisation – see notes for Chapter 4, The Structure of Magic - '*...chairs change slowly and undramatically, while meetings change more quickly and dramatically.*'

Nominalisations are of course useful. They allow us to use just one word for a wealth of experiences, meanings and distinctions. De-nominalising is helpful when a person has become somehow disconnected from their own influence and contribution to key aspects of a significant situation and, or, has no rich inner representation to guide their future choices and behaviour.

Philosophers talk about the problem of the reification of the world. Language, and our fixed habits of mind and body, enables us to make our world so solid, stable and real. We make life into things. We turn our world to stone and then feel stuck.

In many ways the de-nominalising process is itself akin to getting things moving, breathing life, lightness, flow and sense of connectedness into everyday situations. It wakes us up to our own impact and influence in the world and to the potential for change.

Some nouns are somewhat complicated to turn directly into verbs and can sound clunky. There is sometimes a bit of art to finding a way of asking the de-nominalising Meta Model question *"How (specifically) are you X ..ing?"*

This question of course is a form of modelling. How is someone currently functioning, processing, choosing etc. in this context? How are they doing it? You are now working with the Meta Model pattern of Unspecified Verbs as well as presupposing that there are other choices.

Exercise 1 - Nominalisations

- Coach, client and Observer settle into open, connected, receptive states in which both can slow their breathing and slow down the process.

- Client offers their problem statement

- Coach turns Nominalisation into appropriate Verb structure X.

- Coach asks question *"How are you X..ing, specifically?"* or the nearest rapportful equivalent question.

- Coach gently, slowly, spaciously helps to keep client focused on answering this more process-type question, eliciting information on external behaviours, internal pictures, words etc. – like a behavioural and VAK strategy elicitation.

- The client tends to become aware now of the choices they have been making in the situation, as well as the quality of information they have been referencing.

- The coach can gently help with this by repeating and mirroring key elements of the clients' answer. The coach is also trying on the client's strategy, modelling from 2nd position.

- After the client's current strategy has been made more explicit, pause and make space for the client to comment on their own learning.

- The coach then invites the client to identify their related goals and desired state - *"What do you want? What's your goal, outcome, intention in this situation now?"*

- Coach calibrates in this process to ensure client identifies a wide range of resourceful and ecological choices.

- Coach asks *"What does **this** way of experiencing this situation now make more possible?'*

- To build more skill and awareness, review the exercise from all three perspectives in the group. Become aware of the experiential and perceived differences between the 'abstract noun' and the 'active verb' descriptions in the issue or situation.

- Track important submodality changes in the clients representations. Is the issue clearer to them now for example?

- Identify and comment on the other Meta Model patterns which have been spoken or implied in the clients statements and answers.

B. Universal Quantifiers - the pattern of *'all', 'always', 'never', 'everyone'* and *'no-one'* – creating generalisations in the speaker's model of the world.

These are the key words we hear or see that indicate that the speaker is currently perceiving personally meaningful similarities in certain experiences and information.

*It's **always** like this. No-one **ever** listens to me.*

This is the natural human process of creating generalisations. Seeing similarities in people, situations, objects etc., and being able to label them efficiently as such, helps us to manage an overwhelm of sensory information. It's a default cognitive ability that accelerates our learning and understanding of the world. We can rapidly make assumptions about how to behave, what to feel and what might happen next.

If situations appear to be similar it not only helps us to streamline our responses in the present, but also to pattern the past so life seems coherent. We also feed this learning forward to create expectations and to predict the future. It creates a certain kind of automatic programming for us, allowing us to stereotype people, places, things, issues etc. for good and for ill. It's a supremely efficient, energy-management capability, which builds our habits – which of course create our actions and our lives.

When coaching with the Meta Model the coach is working with how the client is structuring their experience; how they are subjectively patterning the data to make sense of their world.

Seeing similarities is a perceptual act, a personalised, rule-based filtering of information. The words we use to describe anything are forms of generalisation. For example to label a structure with a surface as a 'table' is to place it in a mental category or template of all possible 'tables'. It's like saying, *"All these examples are exactly the same and therefore I will respond to all of them in exactly the same way."*

A more slowed down Zen-like coaching style allows both coach and client the space to become more aware of this unconscious process. This also applies to working with other statements and patterns in the Meta Model. The Zen aspect helps us experience how we are always putting our world together to make it make sense and that this is an active perceptual process on our part. This realisation can take us to a place almost beyond words, able to sense and enjoy the actual, uncategorised openness of experience.

There are assumed 'always' hidden in statements in other Meta Model patterns. They are presupposed in Cause-Effects, Complex Equivalences, Modal Operators, Lost Performatives, Presuppositions and Mind Reading. You could spend a whole practice group session just eliciting these and finding out how these patterns hang together. It's always fascinating to appreciate that there is more than one Meta Model process per statement in this linguistic form of modelling.

The Universal Quantifier structure is at the core of phobias, triggers and anchors. *'Whenever X, I respond Y'* contains a world of related Meta Model patterns. It's also the core rule for the 'Matching/ Similarity' meta-programme in NLP and often for 'Big Picture/ Small Chunk' too.

The Meta Model challenge for this 'Universal Quantifier' similarity pattern is to request differences and counter-examples. The invitation is to find examples in the category that don't fit the rules. What might be exceptional and unique, a potential error, a mis-categorisation?

This challenge usually helps to distinguish exact time–space co-ordinates of the counter examples, as well as specifics and details of singular or multiple exceptional occurrences, persons and responses. This allows the client, through new contrasts and comparisons, to re-contextualise and re-categorise their issue. It brings new, important distinctions to the issue and begins the process of enriching the inner representations, generating the new choices, renewing the motivational energy and the sense of possibility.

Exercise 2 - Universal Quantifiers

Q. Always? No-one? Never? Are there any exceptions? Has there ever been a time when X or Y did/ did not happen?

Notice the client's search process which the question provokes and how finding the answer already starts to change their 'map'.

At this point the 'always' or 'never' has often been rendered invalid. The client now has the opportunity to exit the trance state of creating fixed generalisations, and to talk about their issue in a more specific and yet open way. This next phase of exploration involves the coach helping the client find the right kinds of words for the issue, now that it is being perceived as more appropriately contextualised.

In the less usual event of there being no perceived counter-examples then the coach continues as below.

Once the 'problem state' has been specified, the coach can then guide the client into more of an outcome orientation.

- *"So what do you want instead (of the problem or limitation)?"*

- *"What is your outcome now?" "What do you want to have happen?"*

In this phase the coach works with the client to help them articulate and then richly represent their new goal(s). The Well-Formed Outcomes model is ideal for this with it's multiple invitations to somatically sense and integrate new possibilities.

The emphasis in this session is about exploring, revising and expanding rather than solving and settling. The goal of the coaching interaction is to help the client set a new direction and take a step forward. The client shifts to more effective and congruent behaviour. And both of you can sense that something 'magic' has just happened.

A final possible step, in a practice group learning context, is to make a 'before' and 'after' comparison. Pay attention to the key submodality changes and to any physiological shifts in breathing, posture, gestures, degree of muscular tension/ relaxation.

Running the session successfully

- enjoy de-constructing the patterns and understanding how they function.

- maintain the soft, open, slowed-down, spacious coaching mode

- focus on the actual Meta Model patterns and questions, the calibration and rapport, the pacing and leading - don't get drawn into solving or discussing the client's content.

- generate examples from real issues – the client's internal dialogue, when in an unresourceful state is often a rich source of self-limiting statements

- enjoy this more generative, Zen-type state – how else will you use it, practise it, enrich it?

THE FIVE-MINUTE COACH

by
Lynne Cooper

"It is not the answer that enlightens, but the question."

EUGÈNE IONESCO

Biography for Lynne Cooper

Lynne is a highly experienced Executive Coach accredited by the Association for Coaching (AC), Team Coach and accredited Coaching Supervisor. She is also a skilled facilitator, specialising in developing leaders and building teams to create improved performance.

With a background including some 18 years' commercial experience in management roles within private sector organisations, Lynne has subsequently spent nearly fifteen years coaching and facilitating. She holds diplomas in Management Studies, Marketing and Coaching Supervision.

A Business graduate, NLP Master Practitioner and a certified Clean Practitioner, Lynne is one of just a handful of pioneers of the application of Clean Language and Symbolic Modelling in organisations, using this leading edge change technology to enhance understanding, transform thinking, change behaviours, and sustain the resulting improved results.

Lynne is the co-creator of The Five-Minute Coach, a powerful Clean Language coaching model for use across management levels, integrating coaching into day-to-day communications to facilitate generative change.

Lynne is Vice Chair, UK for the Association for Coaching. She is a member of the Association of Coaching Supervisors.

Lynne is the author of Business NLP for Dummies, Wiley, 2008, and co-author of The Five-Minute Coach, Crown House Publishing, 2012.

www.changeperspectives.co.uk

I chose this topic for a practice group subject because it's proved extremely popular with practice groups over the years, not just because I am the co-developer of the Five-Minute Coach and co-author of the book of the same name!

We developed the Five-Minute Coach originally for managers to use on-the-job at work to improve performance. We now find it being embraced by professional coaches, parents, health professionals and more, as it can be used as an effective yet straightforward coaching model. It works really well in small chunks in everyday conversations, helping people consider their outcomes, choose their actions and resolve their own problems.

My experience is that group participants like the content of this session, which offers very accessible and practical techniques that are quick to learn and apply with clients, colleagues, friends and family. It's an ideal practice group subject as it lends itself to a lot of exercises and active participation. It works well for groups of mixed levels of experience, from NLP novices to seasoned practitioners who can weave the approach in with new ways to practise some of their NLP skills.

The Five-Minute Coach is based in Clean Language, one of the newer innovations in NLP, with which not all practitioners will be familiar. Again, the practice group exercises are straightforward and easy to pick up and offer a new way of using Clean Language for those who are already acquainted with it and a whole new, yet accessible, technique for those who are not.

Outcomes for the Session

From this session participants should go away with new additional learnings in the areas of:

- Coaching

- Exploring and developing well-formed outcomes

- Facilitating others to develop action plans

- Clean Language questioning

- Practising, in new ways, a range of NLP tools, models and skills:

    - Sensory-specific definitions of an outcome
    - Calibration
    - Matching and pacing
    - Future pacing
    - Chunking
    - Presuppositions, including: people have all the resources they need

The outcome of the session is for people to have something to take away and apply immediately, whilst learning in the context of their existing NLP skill base.

Background

It's important to introduce the session, provide some background and context and explain what the Five-Minute Coach is, its principles and the nature of the approach. A little background in Clean Language helps to set the scene.

The questions in the Five-Minute Coach are mainly derived from Clean Language, a relatively new innovation in NLP, largely derived from Penny Tompkins' and James Lawley's modelling of the excellence of the psychotherapeutic interventions developed and practised by David Grove. Not all NLP practitioners are experienced in the Clean Language style of questioning so a small amount of set-up at the start of the event speeds up people's ability to integrate the approach quickly and effectively.

You may wish to reassure participants that this is for all levels of NLP experience and indeed for those who are not familiar with Clean Language as well as those who are.

I suggest that you set the context for the session with the following information:

A brief explanation of key Five-Minute Coach principles:

- The coach leads the process, the coachee leads the content of the conversation

- The coachee has all the answers and all the resources he or she needs, and takes full ownership

- The coach is working fully with the coachee's map of the world - none of the coach's thoughts, assumptions or words are introduced to the coachee

- The coach must manage any personal discomfort experienced by not being able to question specifically to gain understanding of the deep structure of the coachee's thinking

- The questions are given and fixed. The coach only has to include something from the coachee's words within the question, as indicated in the structure, to drive the process

Tips – to be presented as a handout or visual aid – for the coach:

- Use only the Five-Minute Coach questions

- Listen carefully

- Repeat the coachee's words

- Take notes

- Ignore the normal rules of conversation

These tips may warrant some further explanation at the start – and may need to be revisited in debriefs throughout the session. Here is some background:

Use only the Five-Minute Coach questions

Sticking with the questions is essential. This can be challenging at times, especially for those with an options meta programme, as the coach needs to supress any desire to ask a question he or she may think is far more useful, or to change the grammatical make up of the question.

Listen carefully

Paying close attention needs little introduction to an NLP practitioner but listening for the exact words (including grammar) of the coachee can be a stretch for some. Calibrating the coachee's voice and physiology will give useful clues as to when and how to ask the next question.

Repeat the coachee's words

The repetition of the coachee's words (where indicated in the framework) is an important part of the process. It helps the coachee to access his or her own deeper structure, often resulting in a semi-trance like state, which enables deeper exploration and greater insights.

Take notes

Taking notes challenges some. It slows things down and many NLP practitioners express concern that this will impair rapport. In fact, the reduced eye contact and slower pace helps the coachee to reflect and explore at depth.

Ignore the normal rules of conversation

This session isn't a dialogue and shouldn't sound as such. The coach's thoughts, ideas, suggestion or even desired questions do not fit here. This is purely about the coachee doing his or her best thinking. Further, when inserting the coachee's words into a question, grammar does not need to be changed to make the question sound 'normal'.

The Five-Minute Coach Framework

This is outlined in handout 1 (at end of chapter) which should be distributed.

Exercises and Activities

Exercise 1 - Problem to desired outcome

First, provide very simple definitions of the difference between an outcome and a problem. In the practice group context we want to keep this simple rather than developing completely well-formed outcomes.

Definitions:

• An outcome is something you *want*

• A problem is something you *don't want*

In pairs, allow two or three minutes each way. Total time for exercise including set up and debrief - 15-20 minutes.

Instructions

1. Coachee thinks of a problem statement and shares with the Coach.

2. Coach asks: **"And** [problem in Coachee's words], **and what would you like to have happen?"**

3. Conversation continues until Coach is convinced Coachee has a desired outcome, expressed in the positive.

Debrief, exploring the impact of this Clean Language question, comparing to the more typical question: "and what would you like instead of [problem]?"

Exercise 2 - Chunking up (exploring higher-level outcomes)

Another exercise, once an outcome has been defined, is to explore with the coachee what an outcome will do for the individual. This is the second stage of the Five-Minute Coach process.

First, remind participants of one of the values of chunking up – to get a higher level piece of information. In this context, the coachee has the opportunity to explore what the achievement of the outcome will mean, to engage with that, and then consider whether a higher chunk outcome once discovered is where it is more useful to place attention.

In pairs, allow five or more minutes each way. Total time for exercise including demo, set up and debrief - 25 minutes.

Unless all participants have experience of using Clean Language questions I recommend that you demonstrate the activity to the group briefly before the exercise. Ensure you write all the coachee's answers accurately on a flip chart or white board to model that part of the process.

Instructions

1. Coachee states his or her outcome.

2. Coach writes down the exact words that the Coachee has spoken and then asks:

"And when [outcome in Coachee's words], *then* **what happens?"**

3. Coachee responds and the Coach writes down the Coachee's exact words.

4. Coach then asks:

   "And when [last answer], *then* **what happens?"**

5. Coachee responds and the Coach writes down the Coachee's exact words and then asks:

   "**And when** [last answer], *then* **what happens?"**

6. This process continues until the question has been asked six times, unless the Coachee has started to give repetitive answers or no answer.

7. After six iterations the Coach, using the notes taken, asks:

   "And [outcome in Coachee's words]**, and** [all the answers given to date, in order]**, and what are you drawn to most?"**

8. At this point, the Coachee chooses one of the statements he or she made through the exercise. Some people stick with their original statement; others prefer another statement from their list, representing a bigger chunk outcome.

Debrief, first focusing the group's attention on what happened for them as coachees. How was it to be asked these questions?

Facilitate a discussion about this *before* exploring the experience of doing the exercise as a coach, addressing concerns of those feeling uncomfortable in this new style of coaching, comparing with the positive experiences of being coached in this way.

Exercise 3 - Sensory specific criteria – the evidence of success

This optional exercise is a valuable reminder for practitioners that an outcome expressed in sensory-specific terms is a more well-formed outcome. Additionally, there is a second-position perspective on the evidence of outcome achievement.

First, introduce the concept of sensory specific criteria for outcomes and the value of using these to future pace the achievement of an outcome.

In pairs, allow 6-10 minutes each way.

If time, a demonstration of this exercise can be useful. All answers should be recorded on a flip chart or white board, following the discipline of the Five-Minute Coach exercises, although the answers to these questions are not repeated as they are in some of the other exercises.

The questions in the following instructions are best presented as a handout or written up somewhere clearly where the whole group can see them whilst carrying out doing the exercise.

Instructions:

1. Coachee states his or her outcome

2. Coach asks:

   "What will you see, hear or feel that lets you know you have [outcome in Coachee's words]**?"**

3. Coach writes down the answer and asks:

   "And is there anything else that you will see, hear or feel that lets you know you have [outcome in Coachee's words]**?"**

4. Coach writes down the answer and continues this process until the Coachee responds with a congruent 'no'.

5. Coach then asks:

   "And is there anything that others will see or hear that will let them know you have [outcome in Coachee's words]**?"**

6. Coach writes down the answer and asks:

   "And is there anything else others will see or hear that will let them know you have [outcome in Coachee's words]**?"**

7. Coach writes down the answer and continues this process until the Coachee responds with a congruent 'no'.

Then debrief.

Exercise 4 - Action Planning

This is a practical stand-alone exercise that can be done with any outcome for an individual or indeed a team goal. In the context of this practice group, participants will take their latest version of their outcome and work to find out the steps required to achieve it.

Work in pairs, preferably with a change of partners from previous exercises. Allow 10-15 minutes each way. Total time for exercise including set up and debrief - 50 minutes.

I recommend a demonstration of this process to the group. Distribute handout 2 (at end of chapter) first and ask the group to pay attention to the process as mapped out on the handout. Scribe the answers onto a flip chart or white board.

Instructions:

1. Coach asks the Coachee for the outcome and writes down the Coachee's exact words for what is wanted on to handout 2. For example, if the Coachee says: "I want to write and publish my NLP book by December this year." the Coach writes in the handout: *to write and publish my NLP book this year.*

2. Coach then asks the Coachee the second question on the handout in the following form:

    "And what needs to happen for you to write and publish your NLP book this year**?**

    Notice that the 'for you' has been added in by the Coach here. As the outcome was expressed as something the Coachee wanted to do this is a reasonable phrasing. If the Coachee had said "I want a new job this year" the coach may express the outcome in this question as:

"And what needs to happen for a new job this year**?"** It may sound strange grammatically but will work very effectively for the Coachee.

3. Coach then uses this format for the later questions, following the instructions on the handout.

4. Once the final question generates a congruent 'yes', the Coach passes the action plan handout back to its owner – the Coachee.

Note – should there not be a congruent 'yes' in answer to the final question the coach should then ask:

"And what needs to happen for [first thing that needs to happen]**?"** and then cycle through a whole new action planning process for that.

FURTHER TIPS

*   Pace any discomfort experienced by those new to a Clean Language process.

*   Encourage people to move out of their comfort zones.

*   In debriefs put people's attention on their experience when *being coached* before exploring any challenges they had when coaching.

*   Fit the number of exercises to the time you have – make sure you allow sufficient time for discussion after each activity.

*   Finish the event with an exploration of where and when participants might use what they have learned and practised.

Handout 1

The Five Minute Coach Framework

Stage	Purpose	Questions
1	Identifying an outcome	**And what would you like to have happen?**
2	Choosing the best outcome	**And when** [outcome in coachee's words], **then what happens?** **And when** [last answer], **then what happens?** (Repeat question, with each answer, until no new answers emerge) **And** [outcome] **and** [recap all answers], **what are you drawn to most?**
3	Discovering more about the outcome	**And when** [new outcome], **what kind of** [word or phrase from outcome]? **And when** [last answer], **is there anything else about** [same word or phrase]? **And when,** [last answer], **where is/are** [same word or phrase]? **And when** [last answer], **whereabouts** [last answer]? **And** [last answer]. **Given what you *now* know, what would you like to have happen?**
4	Action planning	**And what needs to happen for** [final outcome]? **And is there anything else that needs to happen for** [final outcome]? (Repeat question until you hear first 'no') **And** [final outcome and recap every action point] **And is there anything else that needs to happen for** [final outcome]? (Repeat question until you hear second 'no') **And** [final outcome and recap every action point], **and what needs to happen *first*?** **And can** [previous answer]?
5	Motivate to act	**And when** [first thing], ***then* what happens?** **And when** [last answer], ***then* what happens?** (Repeat until coachee is in a positive state and seems keen to act) **And is that a good place to stop?** (Hand over notes)

··

Handout 2

The Five-Minute Coach stage 4 action planning

Outcome:

Ask the Coachee the following questions:

And what needs to happen for [outcome]**?**

And is there anything else that needs to happen for [outcome]**?**
(Repeat question until you hear first "no")

And [outcome and recap every action point]. **And is there anything else that needs to happen for** [outcome]**?**
(Repeat question until you hear second "no")

And [outcome and recap every action point], **and what needs to happen first?**

And can [previous answer]**?**

Pass notes back to Coachee

··

FINDING WORK THROUGH RELATIONSHIPS

by

Chris Howell

"Nothing liberates your greatness like the desire to help, the desire to serve."

MARIANNE WILLIAMSON

Biography of Chris Howell

Chris Howell CPCC ORSCC has over 30 years experience of consulting, facilitating and coaching. He has consulted on numerous successful information technology and business organisation changes. He has managed at senior level within global business critical change programmes and now coaches leaders and teams internationally. His clients include central and local government, non-profit, finance, manufacturing, insurance and well-known international corporations.

Chris is a certified Co-Active and Systems coach with a background in Psychology, Organisation Development and NLP Training. Chris's specialist research area is the influence of leaders in aligning on vision and values. He is also a certified Project Manager.

Chris coaches teams and organisations that aspire to exceeding the potential they can currently imagine, and he coaches individuals who are inspired to be who they are capable of being.

www.peoplesystemsthinking.co.uk

Finding work is both challenging and critical. We are under increasing pressure to ensure we have continuing work that allows us to thrive, both as individuals and as organisations. Time and again people express their pain and frustration at the difficulties of getting the work they want. People who are successful in finding work tend to seek their opportunities and secure work through new or existing relationships, so being competent at finding work through relationships is of growing importance in our world today.

In my own career, I have succeeded in maintaining a company for over 20 years finding all my work through relationships. Through all that time I have observed, modelled and learnt from other individuals who are both naturally and professionally gifted, and masterful at finding their own work through networks of relationships. It is my privilege to share here some of what I have discovered.

How do we find work?

Whether an individual is looking for a job, freelance opportunities or even working for a larger organisation, finding work is most effectively achieved through relationships. Consider, for a moment, how you normally decide where or who to buy from? For example, if you had some important building work to do on your home, what criteria would you use in deciding which builder to use? One of your criteria is likely to be how much you can trust the builder to do a good job. Yet how could you know of any builder's likely job performance?

Under these circumstances, many people's first step is to ask their friends and associates for referrals or recommendations. Finding work through referrals and recommendations also continues to be very important in business and organisations for the very same reason; when executives are under pressure to deliver they want to be confident that the person they find will do a good job.

How do we find and build the sort of relationships that lead to getting more work? How do we create successful networking relationships and what do successful networkers do that makes the difference?

In this session, participants will generate new beliefs and behaviours for creating networking relationships. Common beliefs, behaviours and qualities of successful networkers are offered for inspiration. Participants will have the opportunity to describe, enrich and practice a new story for themselves, to help build their own networking relationships.

This practice group session focuses on achieving outcomes through generative discussion and through practical experience. For each exercise there is a first step of discovering awareness in oneself before enriching the experience through sharing and listening.

Menu of key tools, models and skills

From an NLP perspective, various models inform the process and assist in developing the neural connections, thereby generating the positive associations that will enrich and anchor new desired behaviours.

- Neuro-Logical levels

- Well formed outcomes

- Modelling successful networkers

- Self-modelling

- Belief structures; cause-effect and equivalence

- The Disney model; Dreamer, Realist, Critic

- New behaviour generator

- Anchoring

Exercises and Activities

Exercise 1 - Finding Negative Associations

Outcomes for exercise:

- To acknowledge the pain or difficulties currently experienced in networking. To identify limiting beliefs that hold back networking success and to recognise that there is a choice through having that awareness.

- To generate a networking success story and to deepen and enrich the sensory experience of the story.

- To identify useful beliefs from the story that facilitate networking success.

Working in pairs, allow 10 minutes each way for step 1, 10 minutes each way for step 2, and 10-20 minutes for group discussion. A total of 30-40 minutes.

Part One

Find negative associations that are holding you back. Working individually, take 2 minutes to consider your responses to these questions:

- What does finding work through relationships mean to you?

- What are your worst nightmares in finding work through relationships?

- What beliefs do you have about yourself and about building relationships that can make it difficult to find work through relationships?

Now take each question one at a time in sequence. If possible, share your responses with a partner. When we verbalise and share our thoughts and feelings, this creates connections with different parts of the brain. When we listen to the thoughts and feelings of another, our brains create associations with our own similar experiences so further enriching and deepening our own awareness in the context. This process of sharing our experiences and of listening to the experiences of others is used throughout these exercises.

Sharing experiences with a larger diverse group can increase the range of possible behaviours available to us. The added variety of sharing within a larger group can help us to discover, for example, that nearly everyone in a networking situation has a range of similar negative beliefs. Nearly everyone is nervous, yet we can also find there are people for whom this nervousness is a positive resource. Not everyone choses to listen to their negative beliefs. There are people who make a choice to listen to their positive beliefs, which is a choice available to us all.

Part Two

Start to generate a shared pool of networking success stories. Generating a success story allows us to create a positive vision of how we would want things to be. As we share and listen, our own story becomes enriched, more detailed, more elaborate. We also learn from the consequences that other people describe and can evaluate what that means for us. As we add detail to the story, particularly when the detail is observable and sensory, the story becomes more believable, more real and more achievable. Sensory details are from the physical environment, what we are doing and how we are doing it, through what we see, hear and feel. Consider then, individually at first, your responses to these questions:

- What would you like the outcome of your networking to be? Make a short clear positive statement of the desired outcome you wish to achieve in your story.

- Make up a story of your ideal networking experience and the best possible outcome. Allow the story to describe what happens as you go through the experience in terms of what you personally would see, hear and feel.

- What positive beliefs need to be true about yourself, about networking and about other people, for the story of your ideal outcome to come true?

Now take each question one at a time in sequence. If possible, share your responses to each question with a partner. As you are listening to your partner, ensure that they have a positive statement of what they want to achieve, that they are telling their story from first person, using 'I' rather than 'it' or 'you', and ask them questions to help them associate with the story, noticing what they see, hear and feel.

Note: It's not necessary for a story to be right, nor for it to be real. It is still just a vision and it is important for the person to feel that it is their own believable story of success and one that resonates for them and is desirable.

Even more can be gained through sharing and developing these stories with a larger group. (Through sharing with a larger group, we can learn from the variety of stories and experiences. It can then be easier to identify a broader range of different positive beliefs about networking.) Ensure that all these positive beliefs are captured and recorded so that all can see. Even when similar beliefs are expressed in slightly different ways, it is useful to capture every variation as each variation can inspire different interpretations.

Exercise 2 - New Behaviour Generator

Outcomes for exercise: To generate new behaviours for the chosen situation.

Working in pairs allow 5 minutes each way for this exercise.

There are two positive beliefs that successful networkers tend to have in common:

"Everyone is interesting."
"Everyone has something of value to contribute, including me."

Part One

Working individually, consider the positive beliefs that successful networkers tend to have:

- How would you behave differently in a networking situation, if these beliefs are really true for you?

- How could these behaviours improve the outcomes of your personal story of success?

Part Two

Working in pairs and taking turns both to explore and to coach, use the New Behaviour Generator to visualise yourself going through your story.

1. Stand up and imagine how you would look, there in the location of your story.

2. Imagine you can actually see yourself there standing in front of you. Project an image of yourself in front of you as if you were watching a 3D movie of yourself standing in that location.

3. Imagine you can see the image of yourself going through your story. Watch as the image of yourself meets people and follows through the story. Adjust your story as you need to so that it is even more compelling, believable and real for you. Notice too what happens if you are able to include the two beliefs from step one.

4. What is your image doing? How is it interacting with people? What might not be working that you can change? Play with what you see until you can visualise yourself achieving your desired outcome.

5. When you can see your image really being congruent with these beliefs and you are ready, step into your image of yourself and take all the beliefs, movements and behaviours into yourself for real. Try out the new behaviours, and notice what you see, hear and feel as you enact them. As you do this, notice the feelings that come up for you.

6. If you feel that you are not yet successful, identify what is missing for you and add what is needed to the statement of your desired outcome before repeating from step 1.

7. Step out of your image and repeat steps 1 through 5, until you are confident that you can repeat any new behaviours successfully.

Part Three

The best test of the new behaviour generator is to use the behaviour in a real situation. Try taking on the behaviours you have just generated in a live situation. Go and use them, meet someone new.

After each time you try out the new behaviours, the learning process is assisted through a little reflection.

Consider reflecting on these questions after each occasion you use the new behaviours:

*   What happened when you used the behaviours?

*   What did you learn about any beliefs you have that are useful with these behaviours?

*   What will you take on and do differently in future?

Exercise 3 - Finding Common Qualities and Values

Outcomes for exercise: To learn from a model of what successful networkers do. To realise the importance of building trust. To add to and enrich a personal strategy.

Working in pairs, allow 20 minutes for this exercise.

There are common qualities and values that successful networkers tend to have around what is important to finding work through relationships:

Self-awareness – aware of themselves and highly considerate of their impact on others.

Authenticity – they have a sense of their own truth and are honest and transparent about it.

Integrity – they have learnt that trust is critical to their success. They build trust by keeping promises, so being true to their word. What they say is what they do, which is critical to building trust for them.

Congruence – they are fully aligned in what they say and do, so the meta-messages align with their words. They believe in what they are doing.

Part One

How do these qualities contribute to success in networking? This question is best explored with a partner, or within a small group. Through discussion, the theme of building trust, which underlies each of these qualities and values, can be understood more deeply.

Common behaviours of networkers who are successful in finding work through relationships:

- **Clear and transparent intent -** transparent and clear about their intent.

- Common examples of intent:

  "There is someone I want to meet"

  "I am looking for introductions to other people"

  "I want to arrange a meeting with you"

  "I am asking for your advice"

"I want to find out what you are looking for"

- **Show interest -** Building rapport, be curious, enthusiastic, caring, open and listen. What is in it for the other person?

- **Create feeling –** People remember feelings. Networkers notice and genuinely acknowledge the other person, they engage in relevant and appropriate communication about the pain they wish to resolve and any positive impact from a resolution. Networkers have, and communicate an inspiring vision. If looking for a job, communication would be about the skills used and the problems that can be resolved through having those skills, with examples of when this was achieved in the past.

- **Give commitment –** Networkers are always focused on what they can give, share and contribute. They explore possibility for on-going connection. They offer and invite, or ask for what they want. They take action to give or contribute and fulfil any promises so encourage reciprocity, yet without implying an expectation of response. If they are given introductions they inform the introducer if a contact has been made.

Part Two

Consider:

- What do these behaviours of successful networkers have in common with the useful beliefs and behaviours that you discovered in Exercise 2?

- What would you like to add to your own list of useful beliefs and behaviours?

Exercise 4 - Refine and Embody New Strategies

Outcome for exercise: To refine and embody the new strategy for successful networking through practice and repetition.

Working in pairs, allow 5 minutes each way for this exercise.

1. Think back to the stories that were created earlier in Exercise 1. How would you like to enrich and improve your story from all that you have discovered in Exercises 2 and 3? Consider the changes that you would like

and play back the story to yourself until you are happy with it.

2. Share your new improved story with your partner. Ensure that the story is compelling for you and has sufficient sensory detail.

3. Stand up and act out your story as a role play with your partner, inviting your partner to step into the role of the other party in your story. (This role play is to allow you to anchor the story in your muscle, so that you can be confident of reproducing it when a real situation arises.)

4. Partners can give feedback and offer coaching to help develop, enrich and deepen the useful behaviours used in the story. For more useful feedback ask your partner to describe:

    What positive impact did you have on your partner in their role, and what behaviours, specifically, might have triggered that positive impact?

    What one thing would your partner suggest you could do differently to increase the positive impact?

    What positive thing would your partner like more of?

Exercise 5 - Rounding up

The closing exercise is a group discussion to take the learning from the session and share what commitment is being made to doing something different in the future. This can be done through each person sharing what they are taking from the session, or even better to ask each person to share what one action they will take as a result of attending the session.

Additional Notes

At the start of the session it is useful to ask participants to express their interest and expectations from the workshop. Some participants may come with expectations that cannot be delivered within the time frame. It is best to clarify this at the beginning. For example, the workshop does not specifically cover online networking, following through after the initial connection, nor getting a job.

The session can benefit from a sense of fun and a little playfulness. This often helps with learning and is also beneficial in reducing attachment to specific outcomes when engaging in the networking.

If there is time at the end then questions may arise about the specifics of finding a job, or for self-employed people finding more work.

Finding a new job:

A few tips that I offer in response to these questions include:

- Have a brief presentation on who you are, skills, strengths, etc.

- Express a clear intent to find introductions to people who might be able to help with advice or other introductions. The meetings are not about asking for a job.

- Have a set of questions to ask that will help you get good advice.

- Manage time well

- If you follow up on introductions then keep the introducer informed.

Finding more work

- Have a brief presentation on who you are, what problems you resolve and how you do it, who you can help, and who you are looking for.

- Intentions as for examples given in the session; to learn more about the person, find out what they are interested in and how you might be able to help them.

BE MORE CREATIVE

by
Jonathan Goldsmith

"Creativity as the conversation between the conscious and unconscious minds."

Biography of Jonathan Goldsmith

Jonathan Goldsmith is a certified NLP Trainer, Coach and Psychotherapist. Jonathan works with individuals in his private practice for one-to-one therapy and coaching and with businesses and organisations he works as a coach and trainer. In 2013 Jonathan's company Be More You launched the Be More Creative project which is a pioneering initiative bringing together high-functioning creative people to expand, enrich and experiment with their creativity.

Jonathan was introduced to NLP and PPD Learning by Dido Fisher and went on his first Practitioner course run by Judith in 2011. He went to work in the PPD Learning office shortly after helping to produce and run their training programmes. He left in 2013 to launch Be More You.

Judith and Jonathan started working together again in 2014 and together they have a new vision to develop and inspire those people in the worldwide field of NLP who want to acquire expertise and mastery in NLP.

www.bemoreyou.co.uk

Creativity is, as any good NLP-er should know, a nominalisation! It is a process rather than a 'thing', which is how it is often referred to in our culture. Furthermore, we speak of creativity as an identity level statement, i.e. you either 'are' or 'are not' creative. Looking at creativity from this perspective one can understand how it appears to be something that is slightly elusive, and 'being creative' is the purview of a special bunch of people who identify themselves as 'creatives.'

Creativity exists within all of us; it is a process that we tap into whether we are aware of it or not! The process of creativity, although the form and content of which will be deeply personal and often unique to each individual, is a process of building connection and like all processes it can be modelled and taught.

The best description I have found for this process is that creativity exists as the relationship between our conscious (cognitive) and unconscious (somatic) minds. It is also worth noting that this relationship is often triggered by an external stimulus. So in a way it can be seen as an internal relationship that needs an external relationship to function in. Louis Conzolino (Author of The Neuroscience of Human Relationships) has a theory that inside of us are 'Social Synapses': Synapses that are only activated in an external relationship and I think that creativity is an example of this. Of course in NLP we have had this idea for a while (as 3rd Generation NLP) through the work of Robert Dilts, Judy Delozier and of course Judith Lowe, referred to as the 'field mind'.

I have also drawn from the work of Iain McGilchrist and his seminal book 'The Master and his Emmisary' which for me offers one of the best descriptions of how our left and right parts of our brains interact with each other, how this relates to what we describe as the conscious and unconscious minds and how the brain connects to the body. Like all maps I use this one because I find that it provides a useful description and helps ground the work I do on creativity with a theory of how we have evolved as humans.

When designing this practice group I worked with an artist on a stop-frame animation presentation to go alongside it as I wanted to experiment with both my own creative process rather then come up with another powerpoint presentation. I was also curious to see how an artist would interpret my ideas and bring them to life. I have included in this chapter some of the stills from the animation which will explain why my diagrams look like they do!

The promise of NLP as laid out in Frogs into Princes by Richard Bandler and John Grinder was to make the world a more 'groovy' place and I think that giving your participants the tools to allow them to be more creative in their lives is fulfilling part of that promise.

Outcomes for the session

At the heart of this practice group is the opportunity for the participants to model each other's creative process through embodied (somatic and cognitive) metaphor and to allow the participants to generate how this will give them more choice and flexibility in their own creative process.

Additionally this session offers the chance for participants to experience that:

- Creativity is a process that exists in relationship both internally and externally

- Our creativity lives somewhere inside our bodies as a felt sense

- We can practise tapping into our creative processes and can practise being creative

- We can experience other people's creative process that can expand our current maps of what it is to be creative

- Finally, participants will discover how to create and use embodied metaphors as a way of connecting our cognitive, somatic and field minds

This practice group can be run over 2-3 hours.

Menu of key tools, models and skills

- Working with how people see creativity. De-nominalising creativity as a process

- Using COACH state as a method to connect our cognitive, somatic and field minds.

- Using metaphor (cognitive and somatic) as a way of connecting to our creativity

- Using Somatic syntax

- Exploring other maps of creativity through metaphorical modelling and connecting participants to more choice and flexibility through trying on each other's models

- Chunking up and down

- Creating a shared creative resource (a 'we-source')

- 3rd Generation 'Field mind'

Introduction and De-nominalising Creativity

I usually start this practice group off by asking the participants to answer the following questions:

Who in the group would say, "I am creative."? (show of hands)

Who in the group would say, "I am not creative."? (show of hands)

I then reframe the question:

Who in the group experiences creativity when Dancing? Singing? Acting? Doing craft work? Cooking? Drawing? Writing poetry? Doodling? At work? At home? As a parent? As a child?

I carry on asking variations on the question "How do you experience creativity?" until everyone in the group has raised their hands at least once!

I then talk about the fact that you cannot either 'be' or 'not be' creative. Creativity is a process that is experienced in a variety of different formats as described by the group.

I then introduce the idea that one description of this process is:

'Creativity as the conversation between our conscious and unconscious minds'

What are the Conscious and Unconscious Minds?

At this point I introduce the work of Iain McGilchrist and talk about the differences between how our left and right hemispheres of our brains work (see notes in further comments about this).

Below is an example of a slide that I have used to talk about the differences in how the left and right hemispheres of our brains process information. I introduce the idea that if creativity is the 'conversation between our conscious and unconscious minds' the other way that we can look at creativity is as: "whole brain thinking" utilising both left and right hemispherical processing. You can then say that another way of looking at the conversation between our conscious and unconscious minds is to have both conscious awareness and somatic awareness

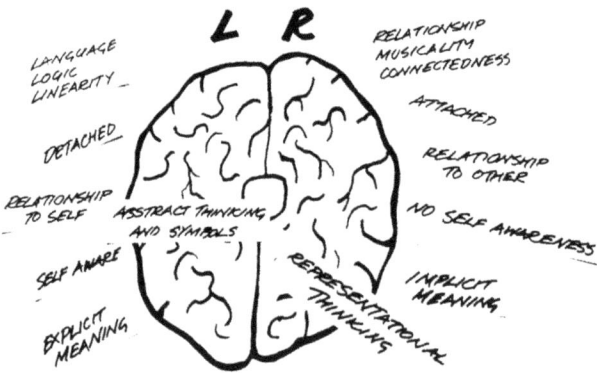

I then go on to discuss that we have multiple intelligences in our body especially in our 'heart minds' and our 'gut minds' and that the right side of the brain is more connected to these multiple intelligences. I also bring in the

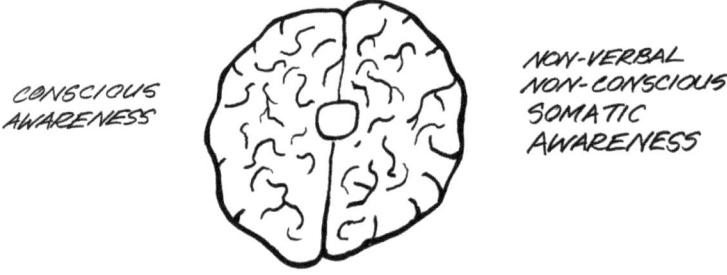

idea that if creativity is 'whole brain thinking' and our right hemisphere is more connected to these multiple intelligences, then creativity is also 'embodied thinking'.

Exercise 1 - Creativity as embodied thinking

At this point I take the group through a COACH state meditative exercise, as this a great tool to align the somatic parts of us with the cognitive parts of us and can give the participants a felt sense of what 'embodied thinking' is:

1. Take some time to get centred. Feel your feet on the floor; bring your awareness up to your gut, the centre of your gravity; allow your awareness and breathing to drop into this place. Say to yourself, "I am present".

2. Allow your awareness to move up to your heart. Say to yourself, "I feel open, open to myself and open others".

3. Allow your awareness to move up to your head. Say to yourself, "I feel awake and aware".

4. Allow your awareness to feel all three areas of gut, heart and head. Say to yourself, "I feel connected".

5. Now allow your awareness to move beyond and through all these areas of intelligence knowing that you can hold all of this within your awareness.

6. Now tune into your sense of your creativity, perhaps in one of the ways that we spoke about earlier. Where does this live inside you? Tune into this sense of your creative process and allow your hands to move to where you currently experience it. Does it have a shape, texture, movement or colour?

Calibrate the group's experience and allow them to enjoy tuning into their sense of their creativity. Then bring the group's awareness gently back into the room and start a discussion on their experiences.

It's important to use your calibration skills to pace the group experience when taking them through this exercise, allow time for everyone in the group to have a felt experience at each step. Eliciting a group trance takes practice and different participants may have different processing speeds at each step. Make sure that you allow enough time to bring the whole group with you.

Exercise 2 - Creating and using metaphor as a part of a creative process

Introduce the idea that creativity exists within an external relationship as well as an internal one referencing back to some of the ways that the group experience their creative process.

I may highlight that dancing takes music, cooking takes ingredients, art takes an easel etc.

I introduce the idea that another type of creative relationship is the relationship between two people:

I also introduce the idea of mirror neurons and the idea of evolution of the social synapse, and that one way we can explore the internal and external relationship is through the use of metaphor.

Metaphors engage both the left and right side of our brains as they have both an implicit and explicit meaning and lead to having a whole-brain embodied experience, both somatic and cognitive.

I then demonstrate the following exercise with one of the group with me playing the part of Person B.

1. A and B face each other. Both access COACH state.

2. When ready, they both say, **"I'm present and I'm ready"**.

3. A tells B something about one of the ways A currently experiences their creativity, in 30 seconds or less.

4. B breathes in A's words and experience and finds a place inside themselves where that information resonates. B allows a metaphor to form - pictures, sounds, movement.

5. B says to A, **"As I hear you talk about your creativity, I experience it as ...."** B offers A this metaphor with words and movement.

6. A breathes in B's metaphor and experiences how it resonates.

7. A tells B how they now experience their creativity, in 15 seconds or less.

8. B breathes in A's words and experience and finds a place inside themselves where that information resonates. B allows a metaphor to form, updating or refining the previous metaphor.

9. B says to A, **"As I hear you talk about your creativity, I experience it as ...."** B offers A their metaphor with words and movement.

10. A now says something about their own creativity in five words or less.

11. B breathes that in, notices where it resonates, and allows a metaphor to form, transform or update.

12. B says to A, **"As I hear you talk now, I experience that as ...."**

13. A thanks B.

Now swap roles for the next round. (B becomes A)

In pairs, this will take 10-15 minutes a round to complete the exercise with both people being person A. (20-30mins in total).

This exercise gives participants the experience of engaging both their cognitive and somatic minds in a creative process. So when Person A says, "I experience my creativity as x", this becomes the relational trigger for Person B to engage their own creative process, setting up the pathway for the next exercise.

I then bring the group back to debrief.

Questions that I would ask are:

1. What was the experience like for you in each role?
    (This question takes the experience into sensory-based evidence)

2. What was your awareness of the process you used to come up with a metaphor?

Using the NLP Representational Systems, how would you structurally model this process?

The representational systems are:

V – visual

A – sound

K – kinaesthetic

O – olfactory

G – Gustatory

We can further differentiate these as, either internally or externally experienced. We describe this, using abbreviations, for example, Ae, for Auditory external, or Ai for Auditory internal.

So B will take in the words of A (Ae).

This may lead to a kinaesthetic response (K+/-)

Which leads to a movement (Ke)

And a picture (Vi)

For another participant it might be Ae>Vi>K+>Ke

Where could you use this process?

You can lead the group to chunk down to behaviours that can be generated or to chunk up to beliefs or values elicited around their creativity.

Below are some suggestions of how this exercise has been used by previous participants:

- Creating emotional resonance: Touching into the experience; letting ideas into the body; creating an emotional connection to cognitive. If you are working on an idea that you want to have emotional resonance, sense where it touches you. For example you may want to create a heartfelt feeling. Does the idea resonate in the heart for you and your team? Or is it in the gut? Play around with utilisation of language and metaphor until it gives the 'right' feeling that you want to achieve.

- If you need to explore an idea in a team, explore how people experience the idea through using Metaphors. Get each team member to develop a metaphor for an idea, project or plan. This can give you insight into different perspectives and you can explore multiple team perspectives.

- Start to think about how you can create shared Metaphors for projects or pitches. What would it be like for the whole team or group to utilise the same Metaphor for an idea?

I would also like to mention the idea of Sponsorship. These exercises can lead to people accessing parts of their world that are tender and precious. Encourage the group to give a high quality of attention to each other when working with their metaphors and descriptions of their creativity. For me, the dual role of this metaphor exercise is to allow the sender of the metaphor, person B, to engage in their own creative process, and person A to have someone engage with them, listening to what they are saying and offering a felt metaphor in response. The very act of listening, in and of itself, represents to me what sponsoring another person's internal experience is all about.

Exercise 3 - Using metaphor as a modelling tool

I usually introduce the next exercise by discussing how the metaphors that we use to describe our creative processes, can be a way of entering into another persons 'map'; how metaphors can be a key to unlocking and experiencing different ways to be creative.

Again I may demonstrate the following exercise with a participant, modelling for the group how this can work:

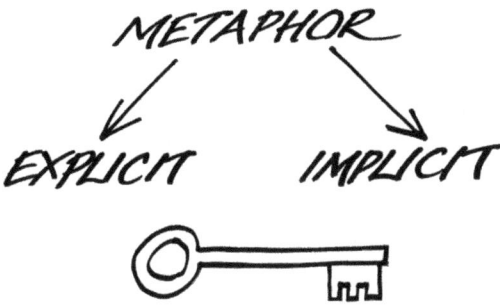

Working in pairs, allow about 5-10 minutes each way.

1. A and B face each other and enter the COACH state, as in the previous exercise. Take time to breathe into your body and find the place in you where you feel you can connect with the other person.

2. When ready, both A and B say: "I'm present, I'm ready."

3. A offers B a metaphor about A's creativity.

4. B breathes that in and uses their imagination to experience this fully. B takes this metaphor and imagines what would happen acting 'as if' that is their map of creativity and notices what difference it makes for them. B now offers something back to Person A about their experience of A's metaphor.

5. Change roles and repeat the exercise.

Once you have completed both rounds of the exercise, find a new partner to do a quick fire version of the exercise, offering metaphors to each other and trying them on.

Bring the group back for a discussion and ask the participants what differences they found when 'trying on' someone else's metaphor.

You can also bring into the discussion the idea that each of us have our own maps of creativity that we currently use, and that by experiencing maps and models different to our own we can actually expand our own maps of what creativity means to each of us.

In the group discussion, the idea is to get the group to realise that by accessing different maps of creativity, new choices become available to them. For example: If person A experiences their creativity as being 'a tall tree in a forest' and person B experiences it as, 'Being a lighthouse on the beach', encourages both of them to explore what modelling each other's process would achieve.

One way of doing this is to ask questions to help participants chunk up and down:

Questions to help them chunk up are:

- As person A, what does experiencing your creativity as 'X' (where X is B's metaphor) allow to happen for you?

- What does experiencing your creativity as 'X' do for you?

Then carry on chunking up by repeating the questions until you have chunked up to beliefs, values, identity, mission and vision. (See Neuro-Logical Levels model in appendix)

Or chunk down by asking:

- What new choices would experiencing your creativity as 'X', become available to you?

- What new behaviours could you generate, if you experience your creativity as 'X'?

- Where and when would it be useful to experience your creativity as 'X'?

For me, this is the exercise where the group can get, 'the most bang for their buck' in this practice group. Modelling and trying on each other's representations of their creative process can resonate on all of the Neuro-Logical levels. It is up to you as the facilitator to elicit from the group how each of them can utilise their experiences. For some, the benefit may be in accessing different beliefs or maps of their identity (from chunking up), for others, it may help them generate new choices or behaviours (from chunking down).

I will encourage the participants to reflect on where and when these models of creativity will be of use to them. If you have a large group you could ask these questions of 2 or 3 members of the group as a demonstration, and then break the group into smaller groups and get them to do this as another exercise. Bring the whole group back together for a final discussion.

Exercise 4 - Creating a shared resource (a 'We-source')

This final exercise is an example of how to create a shared creative resource. Now that people have practised trying on each other's metaphors, I suggest to the group that they play with co-creating a shared map.

I have included this exercise in the practice group as it is a lovely generative way to end, and to give a felt example that the creative process can be fluid and will change depending on the context and stimulus.

You can either demo this or not, depending on your timeframe. By the time you get to this exercise the group should have had enough examples of using metaphor and somatic syntax to experientially try this out without needing to have this demonstrated first.

Before you do this exercise, remind people of the COACH meditation that you ran at the beginning of the workshop and help them tune into their sense of creativity again, and the sub-modalities associated with it. You can suggest that this may have updated itself over the course of the workshop and to take some time to reorient back into COACH and to tune back into the felt sense of their creativity.

Work in pairs and allow about 5-10 minutes for this exercise.

1. Person A and B take some time to orient to each other and to feel a sense of the space between you. When you are both ready say "I'm present and I'm ready"

2. Person A in COACH tune into where you feel your creativity inside of you, allow it to express itself as a movement, demonstrate the movement to person B.

3. Person B do the same and then show your movement to person A.

4. Person A mirror some part of person B's movement and add to, or extend it with something of your own.

5. Person B mirror some aspect of Person A's new expression and add to, or extend it with something of your own.

6. Repeat this process several times, then begin to move at the same time, feeling the energy or 'field' that connects you and find the movement that represents your shared sense of your creative field. When you find a shared movement that feels congruent for both of you, allow the movement to slow down and then stop.

7. Person A and B each come up with a metaphor for what this new movement is like for you and your creative process. Discuss how you can bring this back into your own map and what choices it opens up for each of you.

An optional step would be for the groups of 2 to join another group to make a 4 and to repeat the exercise again seeing what new experiences are generated.

Bring the group back for a final discussion, paying attention to the potential of chunking the experience up the Neuro-Logical Levels into beliefs and values, identity etc. or chunking down into new behaviours and contexts. I also use this final debrief as a chance to anchor new changes or possibilities that present themselves in the group discussion. Finally finish with hugs, applause, cake, tea and whatever else you personally like to end your practice groups with!

Further comments to create an enjoyable and successful learning workshop as a whole.

- When framing the differences in our left and right brain processes as mentioned I have drawn from the work of Iain McGilchrist. For me he has provided the most accurate map of how these different parts of our brain function. It's worth noting that there are a lot of pop-psychology models of left and right brain thinking left over from the 70's that are factually incorrect yet still referenced within our culture. If you would like to learn about McGilchrist's work before you run this practice group, his book, The Master and His Emissary, would be a great starting point. There are also some great films on Youtube.

- When working with an individual's creativity I think it is important that any description or metaphor that arises will only be one way that they currently experience their creativity in that moment. I think there is a danger that if incorrectly framed people may have the impression that their creativity is fixed in form. My experience in working with people's sense of their creativity is that it has the capacity to be fluid and change due to factors such as internal state, external context, group dynamics and what is stimulating the creative process. This is another reason why I like to overtly use metaphor when talking about creativity; talking about an internal process is to a degree, metaphorical. Allowing that in different time/space coordinates and in different contexts can help this change.

- I have run this practice group in a variety of different contexts for both those who are NLP trained and those with no NLP training, I think if you are producing this as part of an NLP practice group you can be more overt as to the NLP elements.

- It will be up to you to pace the group through the initial frames. For me the idea is to ground the more experiential exercises in a solid theoretical base. If you feel that your group is already familiar with McGilchrist's work, or has a good knowledge of mirror neurons, feel free take those elements out.

- This practice group represents for me some of my on-going personal and professional research into the area of creativity. I have thoroughly enjoyed this process and find that helping people connect into, and build a more conscious practised sense of, what it is for them to be more creative is an honour and a pleasure. Enjoy yourself and have fun!

(With thanks to Dido Fisher who worked with me on some of these tools and to Robert Dilts and Judy Delozier who developed the 'we-source' exercise and for Robert Dilts and Stephen Gilligan for their on-going work on COACH state).

STUDY SKILLS FOR ALL AGES AND ALL OCCASIONS

by
Paddy Bergin

*"Before you think about something,
think about how you
want to think about it."*

ANON

Biography of Paddy Bergin

I studied photography at Art College and then worked in advertising and I currently have a Photo Library on the Internet.

Later I worked in the music industry where I managed a 24 track recording studio and a Punk Band.

I started training in NLP in 1990 and began working as a coach in 1993 and now work as a NLP Coach and Trainer with individuals and organisations. I also train and teach Aikido and am currently a 5th Dan Aikido student and Instructor.

www.paddybergin.co.uk
www.paddyberginphotos.com
paddybergin@hotmail.com

NLP practice groups have traditionally been offered by NLP training organisations or by groups of trained NLP Practitioners getting together to provide some access to NLP experience in their local area.

Over the years I have been lucky enough to take part in practice groups presented by some of the world's most experienced NLP trainers including Richard Bandler, Judy Delozier, Charles Faulkner, Robert Dilts, Julian Russell, Tad James, Judith Lowe and Stephen Gilligan.

Trainers often provide their facilitation services to a practice group to help people experience some NLP for a couple of hours, whether participants are new to the field, newly qualified Practitioners wishing to practise their NLP coaching skills or more experienced Practitioners learning about new applications. This practice group session is about learning; more specifically it is about learning how to learn.

Gregory Bateson suggested that there are different levels of learning. In the context of study skills, I work with these three levels:

Learning I - takes place when we study the techniques and take in information about the subject we are studying.

Learning II - takes place when, with time, we learn how to learn more effectively.

Learning III - takes place when we learn about (the purpose of) learning to learn.

At school we were given a continuous stream of information - verbally, through books and nowadays via computers. In Primary or Junior school we learned through all our senses, through activities such as stories, demonstrations, singing, dancing, playing with colours and water. For most of us however, as soon as we moved on to senior schools, teaching methods changed dramatically and information was presented to us verbally and through the written word. We were not introduced to tools for learning, nor shown how to learn.

Later I spent many years working in Colleges and Universities, using NLP skills to enhance and transform students' capacity to learn. Many of the other lecturers would tell their students: "Go and see Paddy, he does weird things."

They didn't really know what I was doing but they knew it worked! I am glad to say that some of these NLP strategies are now slowly being adopted in schools and universities.

This practice group session introduces some ideas and methods that can be used in any context of learning.

Outcomes for the session

To explain the differences between the levels of learning and introduce the idea that people can improve how they learn.

Many ideas in this session are rooted in NLP modelling and are backed up by research. I want people to understand that there is no such thing as a good or bad learner. This is a confusion of Neuro-Logical levels. Learning is a process, something we engage in by utilising various tools and techniques to learn about something and then be able to do it. In other words it is not about who we *are*, i.e. a learner, it is about what we *do* in order to learn.

NLP modelling has provided ways to understand how some people are able to learn excellently, by presupposing that it is not because of some innate talent they have, but more about what they are doing. In other words, *how* they are studying.

Study skills are the strategies or tools we utilise in order to learn. The practice group title presupposes that there are universal methods or principles that are necessary to learn anything effectively.

Learning how to learn

The senses

We absorb information from the world around us through our senses:

- Visual (seeing)

- Auditory (hearing, speaking, internal dialogue)

- Kinaesthetic (feelings which include emotions, external feelings such as rough, smooth, hot, cold, wet and dry, movement and balance).

- Olfactory (smell)

- Gustatory (taste)

We use all of the representational system or modalities and typically people will mostly use one or two of them more than the others. Most of us have a preferred modality as our default. Nobody is a visual or kinaesthetic learner exclusively. The more we develop the use of all of the representational system the more vivid the experience is, which can help in study, learning and memory.

Meta programmes

The meta programmes that drive our motivational preferences are also involved when we are learning:

Motivation - towards and away - We either move away from problems, avoid difficulties or we are motivated towards what we want, our goals.

General and Specific - (big picture and detail) - Some of us are more comfortable dealing with large chunks of information and pay less attention to the detail. Others pay attention to detail and need small chunks of information first.

Similarity and Difference – Some of us will notice what is the same about things and others will look for the differences. Of course both are usually present.

Options and Procedures – Some people are good at following set ways to do things and others like alternatives to choose from.

Internal and External – It is important for some people to decide for themselves; others will take their standards from the outside, seeking direction and instruction from others.

Most people have a bit of both of each of these styles, whilst some operate at one of the extremes.

Four Stages of Learning

In order to learn something we have to do it over and over, gradually getting better at it until we no longer have to think about what we are doing: we can do it automatically. It is said that the path to mastery in any field requires 10,000 hours of practice.

The four stages of learning:

1. **Unconscious incompetence** – we don't know what we don't know; we haven't tried this behaviour yet.

2. **Conscious incompetence** – we have begun to learn to do something and have discovered that we don't know how.

3. **Conscious competence** – after some practice we are beginning to get the hang of it.

4. **Unconscious competence** – continual practice has led to the point where we have got it 'in the muscles'; we do not have to think about what we are doing: it has become automatic.

Stage 2 is the area that most of us find difficult because the experience is all new. We have to deal with and put together, a lot of new pieces of information consciously until we begin to reach a certain level of competency. Stage 2 can feel uncomfortable, as it can sometimes be the stage at which people experience confusion because of information overload. It is also the stage at which the most learning can be gained through perseverance. Confusion is not a state of 'not knowing' but rather new information that you have not yet organised.

Small steps can be useful when learning new stuff to prevent us feeling too uncomfortable. When outside our comfort zone we may retreat or give up as we don't know what to do. 'Failure' is also a learning point. People can get discouraged and stop rather than using a 'failure' to inform the learning and offer the opportunity to improve.

The four stages of learning are not fixed, in that skills are constantly expanded and refined. We learn something well enough for it to be automatic and then add, or make an adjustment to what we are doing to develop further, effectively revisiting stage 2 of the learning process. This amended behaviour gets repeated until it's incorporated and we once more move through the next two stages and become unconsciously competent again.

Learning Tools and Strategies

This section details some tools and strategies I bear in mind when working with this theme. Some may be useful to share, others just to be aware of.

Chunking – according to research by American Psychologist, George Miller, human beings can only consciously track 7+/- 2 chunks of information at any one time. More than that, and we become overwhelmed. Being aware of this allows us to organise information for learning.

Internal States – a key difference that NLP brings to learning is the learning state: curiosity and fascination. NLP tools such as anchoring can be employed to access these states. (See States and Anchoring in appendix)

Mind Mapping – a technique that offers exciting ways of using and improving memory, concentration and creativity enables an accelerated ability to learn. (The Mind Mapping Book by Tony Buzan)

Music – music can enhance study and learning. For example, Baroque music was written to free the soul from earthly matters, with its perfect symmetry and harmony. Research has shown significant improvements in people's ability to study and learn when Baroque music is played in the background.

Metaphor - metaphors and stories encapsulate information in a way that is easy to communicate and to learn.

Beliefs – beliefs are generalisations; they can be both permissions and limitations. Often people have developed limiting beliefs about their ability to learn. NLP tools such as reframing can be used to build more useful beliefs. It can be useful to remind participants that they are already good at learning having learnt to walk and talk in less than two years.

Practice Group Introduction

I start the session with the following story.

There was a very old and wise professor who worked in a University in the Orient. One day he addressed a group of students arranged in a semi circle in front of him. On the floor to his left was a pile of rocks, to his right were several boxes; on the floor in front of him was a large glass jar.

The professor picked up a rock and carefully placed it inside the jar. He then picked up another rock and placed it carefully inside the jar, then another and another until he couldn't get any more rocks in the jar. He paused, stroked his long white beard and then asked the group: "Is the jar now full?"

Lots of hands went up and all the students shouted: "Yes the jar is full."

The professor smiled and said: "Oh no its not."

He leaned over, placed his hand in one of the boxes and lifted out a pile of small pebbles that he carefully dropped into the jar; they trickled down between the rocks until he couldn't get any more in. "Is the jar now full?" asked the professor.

"Yes it is." a few students replied.

Once again the professor smiled and said: "Oh no its not."

He placed his hand inside another box and brought out a handful of sand which he trickled into the jar, followed by another and another until he couldn't get any more in. He looked at the group again, smiled and asked: "Is the jar now full?"

There was a pause and then two students put their hands up and said: "Yes the jar is now full."

The professor smiled and said: "Oh no it's not full."

He reached under his chair and brought out a jug of water. He poured the water carefully into the jar until slowly it reached the top. The professor looked up, smiled and asked: Is the jar now full?

There was a long pause and then one brave student put up his hand and said: "Yes the jar is full to the top and you can't get any more in there."

The professor smiled and looked at the group. He then put his hand in his pocket and brought out a small paper packet that was twisted together at the top. He carefully opened the paper revealing a little pile of salt. Slowly he poured the salt into the jar until eventually a small bump formed at the surface of the jar and once again he asked the group: "Is the jar now full?"

···

There was a long silence until one brave student said: "No the jar is not full."

The professor immediately replied: "Ah but yes it is full to the top now; and we can't get any more of anything in there." He looked at the group, smiled, stroked his long white beard again and said:

"We have put many things in the jar and it is now full and remember this...", the professor paused dramatically, and raised his finger and continued: **"...always put your rocks in first."**

Exercise 1 - Anchoring

Research has shown that 'state' (how we feel) is the prerequisite for effective learning. I demonstrate an anchoring exercise, eliciting a time when the person learnt something really well and with a sense of ease reinforcing the concept of not so much working *hard*, but working *smart*. Another state to go for is curiosity.

You can do this exercise with the whole group or put them into pairs. Allow 15-20 minutes.

Instructions to the group

Choose a state (feeling) that you would like to have, such as relaxation, confidence, calmness, high performance, curiosity, learning etc.

Think of a time when you had this state and in your mind go back to that time. It is important that you are not disassociated, i.e., seeing yourself in the memory, but associated, i.e. experiencing the moment as if you are back there now.

Use all your senses and take a look around and see where you are. Hear any sounds and access the feeling that you had (of confidence, calmness or whatever it was). Maybe you noticed other stimuli like smell and tastes.

When you are sure you are experiencing the feeling you want, stabilise it by holding your forefinger and thumb together.

Hold this anchor (your finger and thumb together) for as long as the feeling is growing and while it's at its peak and be sure to release it before it begins to fade.

···

Do something to break your state or remove the feeling such as move around, shake your arms and body or remember what you had for breakfast.

Now test your anchor by putting your finger and thumb together to bring back the feeling. Know that anchors can be used anytime, anywhere, and no one notices what you are doing. And they are free!

Next repeat this exercise, this time eliciting a state of curiosity (essential for learning). Remember a time when you were curious. See what you saw, hear what you heard and access that feeling of curiosity. Set an anchor when the feeling is at its peak.

Do something to break your state or remove the feeling.

Now test your anchor.

When I present this exercise I also tell a joke or story, which I leave open with a promise to come back to it later, stimulating the state of curiosity and anticipation in the group.

This exercise of course, is not only about accessing useful states for learning but is also a demonstration of the basic NLP process of anchoring for everybody to experience - a tool for life that can be used anytime in any context. Imagine that, one visit to a practice group and you acquire a way of choosing how you want to feel and no longer being at the mercy of your own emotions!

How people learn

We take in information from the world around us through our senses; there is no other way. People may have a preferred system that they process information in, such as kinaesthetic, and they may also have a lead system. These can be two different modalities or may also be the same. So we might 'see' something and then get a 'feeling'.

Exercise 2 – How you prefer to process information

This is a group exercise to elicit each person's possible lead representational system. Allow 15 minutes.

Ensure each person has a handout, or creates a piece of paper, with three columns headed Visual, Auditory and Kinaesthetic, as per Diagram 1.

For the purpose of this exercise we will include olfactory and gustatory in the kinaesthetic system.

Read out a list of 30 words to the group and ask people to put a tick in the column that represents the way they make meaning of the word. You can use your own list, or the one provided below.

Flower	flag	music
bell	smoke	laptop
relaxation	student	dog
water	traffic	sand
colour	window	hand
coffee	wind	comfort
whistle	furniture	fruit
swimming	crumbs	voice
bird	sex	friend
car	book	apple

Explain that it is important to tick the column for the sense they noticed immediately. Ask: What was the very first thing that happened? For example when you hear the word 'chicken', what's the first thing that comes to mind? Do you see a chicken, hear it or smell and taste it?

Hesitiation may lead to a strategy such as see a chicken and then smell or taste it. Remind the group to put only one tick for each word and if any are missed, that's OK, just move on to the next word.

Diagram 1

Visual	Auditory	Kinaesthetic

When all 30 words have been read out ask everyone to add up the number of ticks in each of their columns to gain an indication of how they process information.

When everyone has totalled their columns, ask for a show of hands to see what the preference proportions are in the room.

You may find that the lowest number is in the auditory column. Some people think that in western cultures it is quite commonly the least used system. This is important information for teachers and presenters; because delivering information verbally may not be the most effective method for many people.

Developing VAK Systems

Here are some simple suggestions for beginning to develop the visual, auditory and kinaesthetic representational systems.

Visual

To enhance your use of the visual system use colours. The brain will learn and remember anything that is emphasised in some way using colour, shape or pictures.

Auditory

As a starting point you can sit in a park or your garden and listen out for a bird singing. As soon as you hear one keep listening and you will begin to hear others. Very soon you will be listening to a choir of birdsong and be wondering why you hadn't noticed it before.

Kinaesthetic

To improve your feeling sense become more tactile. Touch things and feel the temperature, roughness or smoothness; feel the wind on your face and what the temperature is like on the back of your hands. Notice your internal feelings - emotions such as happy, calm, angry, nervous, relaxed etc. Where are these feelings located in your body?

What happens when you think of them as communications from your system designed to attract your attention to something?

Stop and smell the roses. What happens when you think about biting into a lemon?

Practising these types of activities on a regular basis will help to improve your ability to use all of the senses.

Using Chunking for Learning

Here are some suggestions for using chunking for dealing with projects and assignments that can look and feel overwhelming to a student.

When I worked in Colleges and Universities students would often say to me that they had a huge assignment to do and didn't know how to do it or where to start. I would ask them, "How would you eat an elephant?"

For a while they would look at me as if I was deranged (that happened quite often!), especially if they didn't eat meat, but in the end they would usually get to the answer "A mouthful at a time."

Coming up with this answer also brought with it a realisation about their own situation with their project. At this moment I would proceed to explain that holding the 'whole assignment' in the mind can cause a feeling of overwhelm. They could see the project more constructively when I helped them break it down into smaller chunks.

> *"A journey of a thousand miles starts with one step."*
>
> *Lao Tzu*

The first step I suggest is to sort out the environment. Do you have everything you need like books, pens, (coloured ones are best), and computer, and is the temperature of the room OK? Once you have all that together take a break, have a cup of tea or glass of water and then go back to the assignment. Thinking about having to sit down for three hours to complete the assignment often puts people off and leads to procrastination.

Think about it differently. Decide to sit down for 20 minutes and work on the assignment. Anyone can concentrate for a short period of time like that and you may find you are able to do a bit longer. Take another break and repeat the cycle, bit-by-bit, piece-by-piece and chunk-by-chunk.

Exercise 3 – Motivation

Typically when learning and studying, people who manage to put things off are seeing all the 'hard work' they have to do and then feel bad. In terms of motivation, it sometimes helps to visualise the assignment finished and connect with the good feeling of satisfaction that comes from successful completion and then each step of the way gets you closer to more good feelings.

You can talk the whole group through this or put them in pairs. Allow at least 20 minutes per person.

| Past | Present | Future |

Imagine time stretched out in a line with the present in front of you and your future to your right. Some people will see their future in front and the past behind - it's OK to work that way also if that is your preference.

Stand in the present. Look along your timeline and visualise yourself somewhere in the future having already successfully completed your assignment. Notice how good that feels. When you see yourself make sure the picture is big, bright and colourful.

Now stand in the present with that good feeling and start the first chunk of your work and keep seeing yourself having already finished and getting more of that good feeling.

Do this for each part of your assignment.

Using Mindmaps

The brain is comprised of billions of connected cells. Linear notes do not match how the brain works which is in a radiant or circular fashion. Mindmapping is a way of taking notes, brainstorming, creating, recalling information, problem solving, planning, revising etc., which is done in a circular fashion so there is a continuous pathway between all words on the map.

See below an example of a mindmap, to find out more please refer to Tony Buzan's book. (See References).

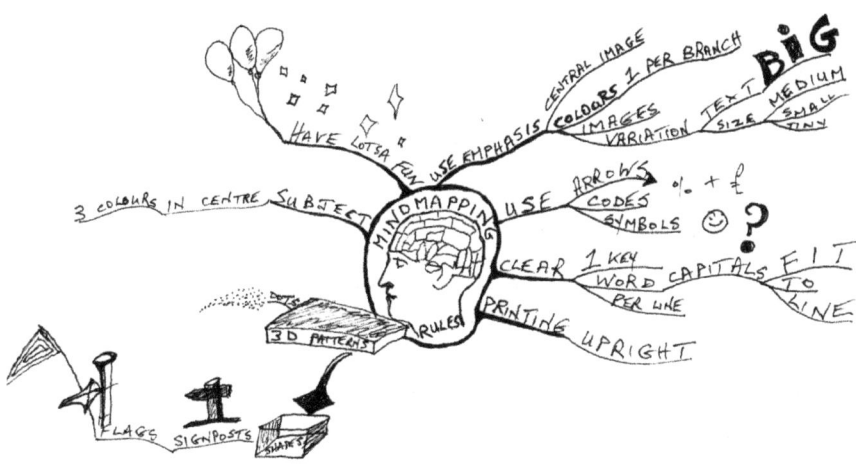

Exercise 4 - Mindmapping

Put the participants into small groups. Allow 30 minutes for this exercise.

Your exercise is to work together and produce a mindmap of everything that we have explored around learning in this workshop. You will find that it is easier to visualise and recall information from a mindmap compared to linear notes in black and white.

Take a piece of flipchart paper and some coloured marker pens.

We will then compare all the mindmaps the group produces.

Place the subject title in the center and draw a circle around it. Write the most important points in colour and capitals on a line branching from the centre. Each branch has its own colour.

When you have done this go around and add another line to the first one, write down the next word for each branch that comes to mind. (This usually happens easily because you have downloaded information onto paper which you no longer have to hold in your brain. This makes space for more information to emerge.)

Continue to do this until you have everything mapped.

When completed compare all the mindmaps the group has produced.

This exercise is both a way of learning to chunk information and learning how to create mindmaps, as well as a demonstration of the effectiveness of the mindmaping tool.

References:

The NLP Workbook, Joseph O'Connor, Element, 2002

Words That Change Minds, Shelle Rose Charvet, Kendall/Hunt Publishing Company, 1997

Training with NLP, Joseph O'Connor & John Seymour, Thorsons, 1994, Page 141

The Mindmap Book, Tony Buzan, BBC Books, 1993

Chicken Soup for the Soul, Jack Canfield & Mark Victor Hansen, 1993

The Magic of Metaphor, Nick Owen, Crown House Publishing, 2001

NLP IN THE WILD

by
Judith Lowe

"An ideal culture is one that makes a place for every human gift."

MARGARET MEAD

Judith Lowe at the British Museum

This is me on our trip to the British Museum with one of the huge statues of winged, human-headed lions currently guarding the Assyrian galleries.

The British Museum is one of my favourite places and it was a pleasure to visit it with an NLP group.

See www.judithlowe.com for my expanded bio, videos, articles and updates on all our current events and courses.

These 'NLP in the Wild' practice groups are a lot of fun. So far we have visited art galleries and museums and been on a riverboat trip. These types of excursions can involve all kinds of public spaces like parks, squares, zoos, special buildings and open contexts, both urban and rural.

In London we are especially blessed to have world-class museums, galleries, historical and culturally significant public spaces and of course multitudes of amazing human beings to observe and model, from all over the world, everywhere we go. There is so much of value and richness to observe, experience and learn in every context.

The goal for these practice groups is to create a kind of generative, collective experience as well as an enriching individual one. Encountering cultural, artistic works of meaning and beauty, locations in nature and the outdoors, and diverse contexts of human interaction, with 'NLP eyes, ears and heart', is a deeply rewarding shared experience. It can promote a very positive, creative group 'field' and energy.

Here are some notes, frames and activities from one of these practice group events - an NLP adventure in a museum. All the 'in the wild' events have been very popular and 'different' and the group has enjoyed being out of the classroom exploring and experiencing an amazing range of artefacts and ideas.

My own preparation involves pre-visits to the locations, to make certain kinds of decisions about the content and the key objectives of the session, as well as to identify essential logistical aspects like disabled access, entry fees, refreshments, timings etc.

I tend to do quite a bit of research beforehand, partly for my personal enjoyment, but also to be a 'good enough' basic guide and facilitator on the day. I usually start the session with some framing, sometimes a brief background history or art 'lesson', as well as the outcomes for the session. I want people primarily to have a rich, personal experience and encounter with the space, the collections, displays, installations and objects, as well as a fun morning together.

An NLP morning at the British Museum

'Curiosity almost universally prevails. Nothing can conduce more to preserve the Learning which this latter Age abounds with, than having Repositories in every Nation to contain its Antiquities, such is the Museum of Britain.' From the first British Museum guide, 1769

The British Museum collection is basically a wonder of the world and offers an essential cultural, historical collection for many successful artists, designers, philosophers, historians, anthropologists and teachers. From an NLP perspective we know that Freud and many other psychologists and healers have been intrigued and touched by sacred objects from the past that resonated for them as symbols of the unconscious. Gregory Bateson, one of NLP's original models and mentors, was also fascinated by art and artistry in different cultures. As an anthropologist he helped develop conceptual frameworks for describing the structures, rules and dynamics of diverse human societies.

The idea of a British Museum itself is also quite a complex one. The post-colonial struggles and debates over the ownership of many of the pieces is most famously exemplified by the on-going argument with the Greek government concerning the repatriation of the Parthenon frieze and statues, formally known as the Elgin marbles.

Ideas of classification and categorisation, so key to psychology and cognitive linguistics, also offer fascinating frames. How are the objects curated and chosen to be displayed together? In the Enlightenment room for example there is a history of the mutability of classifications, as knowledge has become more substantial, scientific and evidence-based. The flint axe heads found near Stonehenge by eighteenth century antiquarians, for example were originally labelled 'elves arrows'.

The actual Museum building too, with its beautiful new courtyard and sense of open space and light, its many galleries, dramatic objects and displays, is also part of the experience of the event - as are the classes of small school children with their drawings and puzzles, and the tourist groups with their own lecturers and guides. It's truly a global powerhouse and meeting place of the world's people and ideas.

....

For the trip to the British Museum we focused on three main topics;

- **Maps and Territory;** the art of categorisation – deletion, distortion, generalisation, - perceptual positions, multiple descriptions, culture

- **Looking through NLP eyes;** meta programmes, submodalities, beliefs

- **Symbolic thought and the Unconscious;** cultural, historical artefacts for inspiration and healing, for living and dying

Useful Presuppositions for this event include:

- Every object, statue and work of art has been created, imaginatively and physically, by human beings and has, or had, a function and a meaning wholly consistent with human life and culture.

- Every belief and every way of living is a human possibility.

- It's possible to 'resonate' at some level with all human artefacts and cultural beliefs: we share the same form, nervous systems and social, personal needs. Our own ancestors made these things and lived in these ways.

- It's possible to identify authentically, and to resonate at some level, with people in other times and cultures to our own, and also, equally authentically, to experience profound 'otherness' and difference.

- The way in which galleries have been created and the objects displayed, demonstrates contemporary forms of categorisation, relationships and meaning – about the world, people and history.

- Time is a construct.

Resources;

- As relevant - various books and guides from the museum. I like to bring a wonderful children's fold-out timeline book which focuses on the so-called ancient world and also shows timescales and comparisons with other world civilisations. As ancient history is a personal passion, I also bring some books on ancient cultures, histories and beliefs. Knowing some background history isn't at all essential to the success of this event though.

....

- Museum maps – there are many levels of guide books and maps available

- Quotes from anthropologists, historians, psychologists in handouts - optional

- Postcards from the Museum's collection

NLP tools and techniques:

- Perceptual Positions – 1st, 2nd, 3rd and 'field' (4th)

- Special aligned soft, open, embodied, aware, information gathering and modelling states - quiet and curious

- Meta programmes (content filters and patterns) and Submodalities (qualities)

- Meta Model – categorisation, meanings, presuppositions

- Messages and Meta Messages – meanings and commentary at another level of communication – for mammalian and 'soft culture' communication it's aspects like voice tone and non-verbal behaviours. For sculpture and 'hard culture' representations, for example of hierarchy and power, Bateson asked *"What if the lions in Trafalgar Square were made of wood?"*

- 'Tetra Lemma' (Stephen Gilligan) - see exercise for brief description

- Beliefs, values, timelines, anchors

Selection of Activities:

Seeing and Sensing – in a soft open state - aligned, quiet, breathing, curious, soft focus - in groups of 4 or 5 create a journey, with distributed leadership, through the galleries, finding and experiencing particular objects.

The logistics for this activity were created by having five stacks of postcards A,B,C,D,E in which all the sequences take people to five different galleries. Each person took one card and then became part of a group composed of an A,B,C,D or E.

The British Museum is huge and I wanted to offer some structure. Card E objects were all in the Parthenon Marbles gallery so we could regroup at the end of the activity. Timing approx. 30 minutes in all. Group members were helping each other maintain a soft open state, with minimal conversation.

This is an entirely subjective experience and also highly contextual. The goal is just to see, to sense and to somehow connect and relate to the object or art in a personal way. It's not a history test and it's ok for some exhibits to be more emotionally, psychologically resonant than others.

Seeing and Sensing – you can curate your own tour for this special kind of appreciation of particular galleries or works. Sometimes it's good to find the quieter spaces as the Museum is usually pretty busy. On one visit we spent time in the Assyrian gallery that displays the lion hunts of King Ashurnasipal ll - exploring the intentions, meta messages and submodalities as well as imaginatively attempting multiple perceptual positions including the king, the charioteers, the artists, the makers, the subjects, and even other tourists in the gallery.

The first stage is a simple, quiet, open, personal encounter with the art; the second can be more of a relaxed patterning using NLP tools and approaches (as above). A third stage might utilise the form and style to create personal meaning and change in some way.

One suggestion from being in this particular gallery, is to create in imagination a kind of storyboard or frieze of personal achievements and aspirations in a similar heroic style and perspective. What does this do for you? Too much?! Does it require adjustments for personal and social ecology? You can play like this with many of the different styles and forms of the exhibits.

A soft, playful approach – more somatic and emotional than cognitive - in these kinds of activities will help to maintain a sense of wonder and respect for the original objects, so as to balance the potential to have a more tightly focused, goal-oriented, instrumental-type experience. Being fully present, aware and open in this context is a pleasure and achievement in itself.

A contrast with this Assyrian frieze might be the Easter Island head, or the Egyptian tombs or the Anglo Saxon Sutton Hoo ship burial or the Shiva Nataraja, Lord of The Cosmic Dance. Ideas, meta programmes and submodalities of scale, materials, movement and the human body in representation are interesting to explore. Which cultures value detail, colour, size, pattern etc.?

"History followed different courses for different people's environments, not because of biological differences between people themselves."
Jared Diamond (from 'Guns, Germs and Steel')

Beliefs and Generalisations – On one of our visits we spent some time in the Enlightenment Room, appreciating the historical and then more personal, psychological aspects of the process of categorisation. As understanding of other cultures and the natural world became more available to western scientists and historians so the displays have been re-organised and re-labelled over the centuries to reflect this.

This is at the heart of how we create, maintain, update and expand our own 'maps' and models of the worlds. Contemporary research in cognitive linguistics, behavioural economics and the neuroscience of perception all demonstrate how we construct and reconstruct our realities. This gallery exemplifies and displays this process and has wonderful examples of confirmation bias, including the story of how people from the west originally thought that birds of paradise were born with no feet, and lived their whole lives in the air. Elaborate stories about reproduction and nesting in the air, even paintings were made of this. Later it was realised that the specimens, all with missing feet, had been simply packed like that for the journey, for efficiency.

One of the NLP activities in the Enlightenment room was a kind of timeline exercise in which people took an event or situation from their past and slowly walked it up the gallery, changing, reframing and updating the meaning and categorisation of it as they went.

Another imaginative exercise is to sense as deeply as possible, beliefs from a culture that are being demonstrated and articulated in a particular gallery or single object. This is also a fascinating way of surfacing, by contrast, our own deeply assumed cultural norms and mental habits. Also finding the 'positive intention' or values behind certain cultural beliefs and inherent in certain cultural objects is often revealing and inspiring.

"Culture is neither artificial nor natural. It stems from neither genetics nor rational thought, for it is made up of rules of conduct, which were not invented

and whose function is generally not understood by the people who obey them."
Claude Levi-Strauss

Using a lighter version of the **'Tetra Lemma'** structure – from first grounding yourself in a 'neutral' and resourceful state -

1. Explore in imagination, using the 'as if' frame, what the subjective experience is for you of believing something in particular that relates to a culture – maybe something about what happens after death, or in the worship of particular gods, or in living a certain way at a particular time and place in history.

2. What is the experience of not believing it or believing the opposite of it?

3. What is it like to hold both those beliefs as true at the same time, the 'deeper truth' as David Bohm the quantum physicist would say?

4. What is it like to believe neither - it's neither true nor not true?

The ability to try on different realities and have mental flexibility about what is, or could be, true and real is core to all kinds of self development and personal growth. It strengthens the ability to go beyond typical polarised true/ not true thinking and to be less attached to particular mental constructs – the map is not the territory.

Vision Quest, Unconscious Symbols and Healing - The feeling of being in the British Museum is really one of wonder. The incredible creativity and diversity of humans over thousands of years is humbling and inspirational. There is the potential there to have some kind of meaningful access to many different everyday ways of life, to empires and peoples long gone, to a wide range of spiritual beliefs and to different ways of relating, as a human being, to the beauty and mystery of life.

It's easy to be touched and moved by many of the works and objects. On a recent trip an accomplished horse rider who had never visited the Museum before was profoundly moved by the depiction and art of horses across so many cultures and over time. This was a personal filter for her and one I had not perceived in that way. For her it enhanced and enriched her own sense of vision and mission in this area.

It is this kind of more unconscious experience of renewal and inspiration that is at the heart of the idea of a vision quest in this museum context.

1. The intention can be set for healing, problem solving, inspiration, creative breakthrough etc. or simply to be touched and transformed in some way.

2. In a state of soft, open awareness let yourself be drawn unconsciously to a particular gallery or exhibit. Stay in deep connection, acknowledgement and relationship with your chosen work, without a need to put your experience into words or to understand it.

3. Allow any meanings and messages to somehow be sensed and experienced by you. Maybe there's a felt sense of a value or intention, or a particular emotion or resource that's part of this experience. Maybe there's a sense of a blessing and a gift.

4. If you wish you may go to 2nd position with the object, and/or its maker and/or its owner. You may go to 3rd position and see and sense the relationship and connection between you and this object.

5. When you are ready and have integrated this experience, acknowledge your choice of object once more and then gently disengage in whatever way is most appropriate for you.

Taking NLP out of the classroom

These types of activities and frames can be mapped across to many different 'NLP in the Wild' events. The main aim is to enjoy the location, the art, the history, the people and the wildlife, and to create activities to practise aspects of NLP out of the classroom.

As with many things in life, keeping it simple is useful. NLP is about communication, learning and change. We have a core toolbox of ideas, models and skills to draw from and much love and laughter to bring to the party. Just being in an interesting and inspirational context, with other NLP ers, with the shared purpose to practise, is already generative and full of possibility. Create some structure and simple activities and it becomes a rich, worthwhile and memorable practice group.

APPENDICES

Running a Successful Practice Group

After you have chosen your theme and content and designed your sequences of engaging and rewarding learning activities, one of the key issues in running a successful NLP practice group is getting the right kind of balance for your group of *task* – learning goals, structured activities, skills acquisition and development – and *relationship* – friendly, fun, social, inclusive.

Too much *task* and it can feel like hard work, too much *relationship* and the evening can lose focus and lack a sense of achievement for people. It's a learning process, so be open to feedback and flexible enough to make any adjustments.

Here are some ideas to help optimise the productive, happy and creative life of your practice group.

Be friendly and welcoming to everyone who attends, have name badges and encourage people to introduce themselves to each other, to mix in, change partners and work in new small groups through the session.

Find out from people, depending on group size, what their level of NLP is, what their goals are for the evening, what their application areas are. This can be done with a show of hands. This allows the presenter for the evening, if you have one, to offer their material at a relevant level. It also gives everyone a chance to feel they can belong and that their unique needs will be met as far as possible.

 Offer tea and coffee before and, or, during a group session. Its an opportunity to get to know people and build the kind of trust and rapport that will help the evening go well. Some of our group also used to go to the pub after the event, though be aware that this may exclude some people.

Suggest people with Masters or Trainer experience partner with newcomers or people with less NLP. We asked experienced assistants to work with anyone who needed extra support.

Have an actual programme and advertise it in advance so that people can see there will be valuable content with interesting presenters, and they can plan to attend.

If you are working more collectively, agree your programme and roles.

Design content that is appropriate for the NLP level of the people there. Most NLP approaches, because they are so natural and intuitive, are chunkable and scaleable for most groups.

Work from the NLP presuppositions – *'the map is not the territory'* means people will have different needs, perspectives, learning styles, results and conclusions; *'you cannot not communicate'* invites you to become aware of influencing patterns and communication feedback loops among and between people; *'feedback and learning frames are more useful and generative than a failure frame'* encourages you to be curious, build distinctions, choices and variety, to enjoy a whole range of possible responses and take learning forward into new contexts; *'every behaviour is subjectively driven by a positive purpose and intention'* allows you to respond at a deeper level to people and to appreciate their values and motivation; *'people have resources'* means people are full of potential and the capability to learn and change.

Calibrate each individual's, as well as the group's, state and guide people into the right kind of learning states for the various activities and stages of the session. Teach people how to be centred, open and aware, how to be rapportful and to calibrate, scale and optimise non-verbal signals and states in themselves and others.

Have the usual basic learning culture of safety and respect for everyone, including awareness of diversity of culture and ability.

Use a variety of demo subjects. Make it easy, safe and worthwhile for people to be part of the demo. Check it's appropriate and ecological for them and others.

Design the sessions so that something definite is achieved and there is a structure that delivers results and learning for people. Give clear instructions about the steps of exercises, and clarity regarding the goals and purpose of them. Have shared, observable evidences for success.

Design variety in content, activities and pace.

Create clear endings, celebrations and goodbyes. Make sure everyone is ok before you leave.

The PPD Learning 'Introducing NLP' Manual

Using the 'Introducing NLP' Manual

Each page of the manual in the appendix, as well as a useful reference for the activities in the main body of the book, offers content and ideas for a practice group in its own right.

Depending on the goals of your group you can also dedicate meetings to practicing the NLP basics and getting the core skills and models 'in the muscle'.

A whole session on Perceptual Positions, or on Framing and Reframing, on Calibration and Rapport, on Representational Systems (VAK) in verbal and non-verbal communication and in strategies, on States and Anchoring, on Goal Setting or on the Meta Model, can be very rewarding and exciting.

Integrating the core Practitioner skills, tools and ideas of NLP on a regular basis builds competence, confidence and flexibility.

If you use the manual in this way as well as the chapters in this book you will have enough material for two years of monthly practice group sessions.

We look forward to your feedback and hope you have at least as much fun and learning as we did.

What is NLP?

Essentially NLP is an *attitude* and a *methodology* for studying the difference between **competence** and **excellence** so that you can acquire the 'best practice' skills in thinking and action in achieving your goals.

As a result of the modelling of high performers and geniuses we have some powerful *techniques* which have been incorporated, in some form, into just about every success-based type of training and development in the world.

NLP - the Attitude

The NLP attitude is embodied in the Presuppositions of NLP.

Key amongst these is *'The map is not the territory'*.

This means that each person creates their own map or model of reality and tends to acts as if their model is accurate and true.

By enriching people's 'maps' of situations through NLP tools and techniques, new choices and solutions are perceived and different, more effective actions may be taken.

Another of the presuppositions is: *"Life and mind are systemic processes'* . This means that we live, think and act in relationship to ourselves and others – with mutual influence and in dynamic feedback.

NLP - the Methodology

The methodology of NLP is the process of modelling excellence through observation and 'calibration', pattern detection skills and the unconscious uptake of behaviour of excellent and effective performers from 2nd position.

NLP - the Techniques

The techniques in the field are the results of the NLP modelling. They consist of step-by-step processes that when followed with rapport and skill create powerful and lasting changes in a person's thinking, sense of possibility and behaviour.

....

Success

"You need only three things to be absolutely successful. We have found there are three major patterns in the behaviour of every wizard we've researched - and executives and sales people.

The first one is to know what outcome you want. The second one is that you need flexibility in your behaviour. You need to be able to generate lots and lots of different behaviours to find out what responses you get. The third thing you need is to have enough sensory experience to notice when you get the responses you want.

If you have those three abilities, then you can just alter your behaviour until you get the responses you want."

from 'Frogs into Princes' by John Grinder and Richard Bandler co-developers of NLP.

1. Know your outcome. Focus on:

- How? instead of Why?

- Useful instead of Right or Wrong

- Outcomes instead of Problems

- Possibilities instead of Limitations

2. Be flexible - if what you are doing isn't working, try something else.

3. Develop your senses to detect relevant feedback.

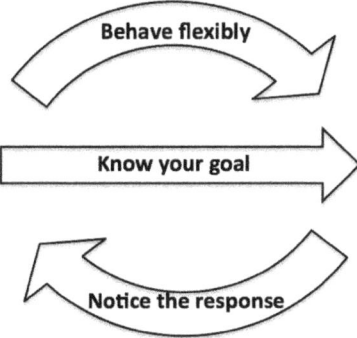

Rapport

Being able to establish rapport with others is one of the key relational skills in NLP. Rapport is a systemic process – more like a dance than a cause-effect linear function. It's not about knowing the content of another person's experience, but about having a 'felt' understanding of how the other person builds their 'maps' of reality and processes information.

Matching and Pacing

Subtly mirroring people's non-verbal communication greatly enhances the experience of rapport. People perceive you as being 'like them'.

* put yourself into a similar body posture
* use similar tonality and rhythm in your speech patterns
* subtly pick up and play back key gestures, expressions, movements etc.

Also match language patterns – identifying and incorporating key words, sensory-based predicates and metaphors.

Pacing and Leading

Leading involves the attempt to get a person or group to change, add to, or enrich their behaviour or thinking process by subtly shifting one's own verbal and behavioural patterns in the desired direction. The basic NLP process of change involves the combination of both pacing and leading. First match and acknowledge existing patterns and then rapportfully and incrementally, help to widen their model of the situation or issue.

Positive Intention

One of the presuppositions of NLP is that all behaviour has a 'positive' purpose or intention. What this means is that all behaviour is essentially purpose-driven in order to accomplish something that the person wants. When a behaviour has negative aspects it is useful to separate the behaviour from the intention which is driving it. Then identify what the intention is – and respond at that level.

The positive intention behind aggression is often protection, the positive purpose behind anger can be to 'maintain boundaries', the positive intention behind 'resistance to change' might be to honour the past.

Calibration

This is the NLP term for noticing and responding to another person's non-verbal responses in a real-time interaction with them. It requires refined sensory awareness and an ability to suspend stock judgments and labels about the other's actual experience. There is high-quality information in these unconscious, spontaneously generated, physical behaviours.

You learn to 'read' the person's body language and relate it to their internal processes and feelings in an individual, specific way. This is achieved by noticing contrast and differences between 'states' - and by detecting significant repetition of patterns in similar states.

Look at:	Listen to:
• Posture	• Tonality
• Breathing	• Tempo/rhythm
• Gestures	• Volume
• Facial Expressions	• Pitch
• Muscular tension	
• Movement/rhythm	
• Blood flow- skin texture/colouring	
• Eye movement patterns	

Calibration is probably the core skill in NLP. It's a prerequisite for rapport and all kinds of communication and interaction with others. It presupposes you are externally focused and open to 'live' experience.

Contrastive Analysis describes the process for calibration exercises in which someone is coached to:

• recall/create memory/state no.1

• then - 'break state'

• recall/create memory/state no.2

The key differences are then noted. This can then be used to label accurately someone's internal experience when subsequently demonstrating similar non-verbal patterns.

Perceptual Positions

This model enables people to sort and clarify different points of view, and the feelings that go with them in relationship to another. The ability to understand a 'communication loop' and the dynamics between people is a powerful tool. You can improve communication, create future cooperation and bring new resources to a situation.

1st Position - Self Associated in your own point of view, beliefs and assumptions, seeing the external world through your own eyes.

Use 1st person language when talking about your self, for example, "I am seeing...", "I feel...". You know your goals, your values – you're standing in your own shoes. Too much in 1st position may lead to insensitivity to others.

2nd Position - Other Associated in another person's point of view, beliefs and assumptions, seeing the external world through his or her eyes.

Use 1st person language when associated in the other person's position as if you are them. You have empathy and appreciation for others' goals and values. Too much 2nd position may lead to lack of clarity about your own identity, goals and needs.

3rd Position - Observer Associated in a point of view outside of the relationship between yourself and the other person with the beliefs and assumptions from both 1st and 2nd position.

Use 3rd person language when talking about yourself in 1st position or the other person (2nd position) 'He is," "She says...", "They are...". You gain perspective or the bigger picture – as if from the director's chair. Too much 3rd position may mean you're disassociated and don't 'get' emotions or the richness of felt experience.

4th Position - 4th position is a perceptual position which involves experiencing a situation with the best interests of the system in mind. It presupposes that you have already taken the other three perceptual positions. It's a 'we' position or 'field' or 'group mind' perspective - a felt sense of membership and sameness that comes from a deep sense of common values and factors which connect people.

....

Representational Systems

As human beings we have five senses – each a representational system, the neurological mechanisms behind the senses. We input, process, store, retrieve and output information using these systems. NLP is based on how we use our senses.

There are five basic ways in which we 'represent' our experience;

VISUAL – seeing – external sights, inner pictures, daydreams, visualisations
AUDITORY – hearing – words and other sounds, self-talk, listening, music
KINAESTHETIC – feeling, touch, proprioception (bodily sensations), emotions, balance
OLFACTORY – smelling - remembered and created smells
GUSTATORY – tasting – remembered and created tastes

Predicates: sensory based words that indicate the use of a representational system e.g. look, see, listen, feel
Accessing Cues: physiological indicators of representational systems
e.g. eye movements, breathing, gestures, posture, voice tonality
Submodalities: the finer distinctions we make within each representational system e.g. a big, bright image; a soft, distant sound; a tickly feeling
Lead System: we use to retrieve information from memory - eye accessing
Preferred System: a favoured or more conscious system – predicates
Synaesthesia: an automatic link from one sense to another

Developing the senses: learn to visualise, hear better, get in touch with feelings, develop body awareness and physical grace

Enhancing rapport, learning and communication: match for rapport, stimulate thinking, create overlaps and translations, pace and lead to a more useful system

Representational System use: relates to capability and preference not identity.

....

Predicates

Visual 'V' - see, angle (perspective), appear, aspect, bright, clarify, clarity, clear, cloud, cognisant, colours, conspicuous, dark, delineate, demonstrate, depict, discern, distinguish, dream, dress up, examine, expose, eye, flash, focus, foresee, glance, glimpse, graphic, hindsight, horizon, idea, illusion, illustrate, image, inspect, look, notice, obscure, observe, obvious, outlook, paint, perception, perspective, picture, pinpoint, preview, reveal, see, scene, scope, screen, scrutinise, short-sighted, show, sight, sketchy, spectacle, survey, vague, view, vision, visualise, watch, witness

Auditory 'A' - hear, accent, alarm, amplify, announce, articulate, ask, boisterous, clear, click, chord, communicate, compose, converse, discuss, dissonant, divulge, earshot, enunciate, gossip, grate, growl, harmonise, hear, hush, inquire, interview, key, listen, loud, mention, muffle, noise, note, oral, proclaim, pronounce, rattle, relate, remark, report, ring, roar, rumour, say, scream, screech, shout, shrill, silence, sing, sound, speak, speechless, squeal, state, static, talk, tell, tone, tune, utter, vocal, voice

Kinaesthetic 'K' - feel, active, affected, angle (fishing), bear, callous, carry, charge, cold, concrete, crash, crawl, emotional, feel, finger, firm, fish for, flow, foundation, gentle, grab, grasp, grip, grope, handle, hanging, hard, hassle, heated, hit, hold, hunch, hustle, impact, impress, irritate, lukewarm, motion, move, muddled, panicky, rub, rush, sensitive, set, settled, shallow, sharpen, shift, shock, smash, soft, softly, solid, sore, sort, stir, stress, strike, stroke, structured, support, tangible, tap, tension, throw, tied, tickle, touch, unbearable, unsettled, warm, whipped

Submodalities

Submodalities are the 'sub-components' of the five sensory or representational systems.

VISUAL - internal images

Brightness (dim-bright)
Size (large-small)
Colour (Black and white-colour)
Movement (Fast –slow/still)
Distance (near-far)
Focus (clear-fuzzy)
Location
Associated/Disassociated

AUDITORY – sounds, speech

Volume (loud-soft)

Tone (bass-treble)

Pitch (high-low)

Tempo (fast-slow)

Distance (close-far)

Rhythm

KINAESTHETIC – feeling/sensation – emotional, tactile,

Intensity (strong-weak)
Area (large-small)
Texture (rough-smooth)
Duration (constant-intermittent)
Temperature (hot-cold)
Weight (heavy-light)
Location

Accessing Cues

Visual Construct

Visual Recall

Auditory Construct

Auditory Recall

Kinesthetic

Auditory Digital (Internal Dialogue)

Note: About one in five people have the whole map reversed. There are many individual variations.

Other Cues			
	V	**A**	**K**
Voice	High pitch, quick, staccato	Medium pitch, rhythmic	Low Pitch, slow
Breathing	High shallow	Mid-line	Deep and low
Face Colour	Pale	Normal	Fuller
Gesture	Pointing up	'Phone' Arms folded	Palms up or towards self

States and Anchoring

A 'state' comprises the on-going mental and physical conditions a person is experiencing. It influences the results and meanings that create our personal world. It directly affects your performance and your ability to learn and be resourceful.

We continuously access and change states as we move through different experiences and contexts of our lives. Mainly we are unaware of having choices about our states... its as if we are on automatic pilot and merely responding to internal and external stimuli.

Being able to influence and direct one's state increases flexibility and creates a higher probability of achieving desired goals – and it's one of the most important things you can do to improve the quality of your life.

Anchoring is one of the most simple and powerful tools for selecting and accessing internal states. It involves establishing a 'cue' or 'trigger' for a specific desired state.

The ability to 'anchor' states allows you to re-access them and use them in a variety of contexts, setting up your own, directed, stimulus-response pathways of associative learning.

For an anchor to be lasting and useful it must conform to certain conditions:

- it must be a pure and intense example of the desired resource state

- the stimulus used (touch, image, word) must be unique

- the timing of the pairing of the stimulus to the resource state must be accurate

- the context surrounding the anchoring experience should be conducive

There are also negative anchors, like phobias or intense inappropriate responses, that you can learn to 'extinguish' and transform with techniques from NLP.

Frames and Reframing

"There's nothing good nor bad but thinking makes it so." Hamlet, Shakespeare

Frames are mental structures that shape the way we see and experience the world – directing our attention and our construction of meanings.

'Glass half-empty – glass half-full.' 'Lucky', 'courageous', 'common sense', 'worthwhile', 'mad', 'scary', 'conflict', - each word activates associations and feelings. Thinking differently requires speaking differently.

"Frames trump facts." George Lakoff, Cognitive Linguist.

Key Frames in NLP

- **Ecology** evaluates in terms of consequences, values, relationships, long-term

- **Outcome** evaluates events and actions in terms of getting closer to goals

- **Backtrack** restates points using other's words, pacing

- **Contrast** evaluates by difference, modelling, contrastive analysis

- **'As If'** pretends something is true to explore possibilities, creative problem-solving

- **Systemic** evaluates by relationship, connections, combinations of factors

- **Negotiation** evaluates by agreement, assumes resources possible and available

Problem Solving Frames

- Outcome (*what do you want?*) v. Blame (*who's to blame?*)

- How? (*how is this a problem?*) v. Why? (*why is this a problem?*)

- Possibility (*what's possible?*) v. Necessity (*what do I have to do?*)

- Feedback (*what have I learned?*) v. Failure (*why have I failed?*)

- Curiosity (*what am I assuming?*) v. Assumptions (*this is how it is.*)

Well-Formed Conditions for Outcomes

(PACER model)

P. State in the *Positive* what you want, a direction, intention? - and not what you don't want.

A. *Achievement* – what will you see, hear, feel, sense? What would relevant others see, hear, feel, sense?

Use your body and your imagination to go forward in time to sense and gather high-quality information about what getting the goal would be like.

Use this 'As if' embodied sensing and testing to build a new possibility as reality; refine and elaborate the goal and test for 'ecology' and wisdom.

C. *Context* – contextualise in time and space – where, with whom etc, do you want, or not want?

E. *Ecology* – testing the whole system for possible consequences and changes. Would you lose anything? What do you want to preserve? What might be short term or longer term, wider reaching effects? What are the values? Is it 'you'?

R. *Resources/ Responsibility* – can you initiate and maintain the process of achieving the goal – self-efficacy, agency, cause-effect, responsibility and resources?

Each condition dynamically shapes, edits, and refines the information for the goal.

NLP Meta Model

Deletions; leaving out key words or information

Comparative Deletions; making comparisons, not stating how, or to what standards of evaluation (e.g. better, worse)

Unspecified Referential Index; failing to specify key actor or object (e.g. they, people, it)

Unspecified Verbs; actions or processes that are unclear or unspecific

Nominalisations; actions, processes spoken of as if they are 'things' (e.g. relationship)

Modal Operators; statements of rules, limits to behaviour (e.g. should, oughtn't, can't)

Universal Quantifiers; broad generalisations (e.g. never, always)

Presuppositions; something assumed, stated as foundational truth

Cause-Effect; assumed, implied causal links between experiences, responses

Complex Equivalence; stated, implied association between experiences

Mind Reading; claiming to know inner experience, motives of another

Lost Performative; value judgments which omit the 'judger' and process of evaluation

....

The T.O.T.E. Model

The T.O.T.E model is one of NLP's key frameworks for organising how people structure and sequence their thoughts and actions to achieve their goals - especially with respect to on-going feedback and learning.

People, either consciously or unconsciously, have goals which direct and give purpose to their behaviour. For each goal the person has some kind of an 'evidence of achievement' in mind – a representation of how success will look, sound and feel.

'T' in the T.O.T.E model is for 'Test'

This 'Test' is a comparison of the Present State with the Desired State – where you are now compared to where you want to be.

'O' is for 'Operations'

These are the actions, steps, cognitive processes etc. that you perform to achieve the goal.

The 'Test' and the 'Operations' together form a dynamic, self-correcting feedback loop that lets you know how to assess your progress and what sort of action to take next.

'E' is for 'Exit' - when your goal is achieved.

T.O.T.E questions:

1. What are your goals? (goal)

2. How do you know you are achieving your goals? (evidences - sensory based)

3. What do you do in order to reach your goals? (operations)

4. What will you do if you are not satisfactorily reaching your goals? (increased variety and flexibility of operations)

....

Time and Timelines

We code events and experiences in terms of past, present and future representations of time. How we organise time can have a significant impact on many aspects of our lives. We unconsciously indicate our 'timelines' through gestures, language patterns and eye accessing cues.

There are two main ways of relating to time:

'In time' – your timeline goes through your body (future in front, past behind) and you are associated in the now. You tend not to be aware of time passing, you aren't so great at planning, possibly avoiding or missing deadlines. Your memories are associated.

'Through time' – your timeline passes in front of your body (usually left to right, past to future) and you are dissociated from the now. You are aware of time passing, you plan ahead, you are aware of deadlines and tend to keep them. You have mainly dissociated memories.

Walking Your Timeline – 'Meta-Position'

Setting up a physical timeline can be a very powerful way to access resources, resolve and learn from past experiences and create a compelling future. You can literally walk along the 'line' of your life, exploring and making changes. You can also switch from 'in time' to 'through time', stepping off the line to a 'meta-position', re-organising your experiences to benefit from the different perceptual frames.

- To enjoy the moment – be 'in time'.

- For time management and planning – be 'through time'.

- To create a compelling future – have big, bright pictures in front of you.

The Language of Time

- 'The dim and distant past', 'looking forward', 'a bright future', 'put it behind you'

- Verb tenses can be used to put problems in the past – 'that has been a problem hasn't it?' 'I had been experiencing X'

Neuro-Logical Levels

This model was developed by Robert Dilts to describe the different levels of learning and change in human beings and human systems. Each level organises and directs the interactions on the level below it like a hierarchy of influence and relationship.

It's useful both as a diagnostic map for problem-solving and also for creating personal and organisational alignment. The skills and approaches for coaching, leadership and influence are different at each level.

Resources & Bibliography

ANLP – The Association of NLP encourages best practice and standards in NLP and offers impartial advice about training. It's a Community Interest Company, recognized as a social enterprise. Karen Moxom is the Managing Director.

As well as lists of accredited NLP trainers and training companies there are links to articles, NLP research, the NLP magazine 'Rapport' and to many local Practice Groups currently running in the UK. www.anlp.org

PPD Learning NLP Practice Group Book Contributors

Paddy Bergin; Extreme Motivation, Stop Smoking Formula e-books
Lynne Cooper; Business NLP For Dummies, and The Five-Minute Coach with co-author Mariette Castellino
Anne Deering; Alpha Leadership: Tools For Business Leaders Who Want More From Life, with co-authors Robert Dilts, Julian Russell
Simon Horton; Negotiation Mastery: Tools for the 21st Century Negotiator

Recommended Essential NLP Reference Library

• Encyclopedia of Systemic Neuro-Linguistic Progamming and NLP New Coding by *Robert Dilts* and *Judith DeLozier.* Free online at www.nlpu.com
• The NLP Workbook: A Practical Guide To Achieving The Results You Want by *Joseph O'Connor*
• The Bumper Bundle Book Of Modelling: NLP Modelling Made Simple by *Fran Burgess*

NLP Related

• Steps To An Ecology Of Mind by *Gregory Bateson*
• Turtles All The Way Down: Prerequisites To Personal Genius by *John Grinder, Judith DeLozier*
• Generative Trance: The Experience Of Creative Flow by *Stephen Gilligan*

PPD Learning - NLP Training

PPD Learning has been a pioneer in NLP in the UK and made a substantial contribution to the development of the field for nearly 30 years.

Our emphasis has always been on providing in-depth NLP trainings that emphasize innovation, skills development, emotional intelligence and integrity.

Our courses and events are focused at the level of mastery and artistry in NLP. We offer a unique and creative pathway to people who want to take their performance, communication, sense of possibility and choice, to more effective levels.

Our Events and Courses

- Masterclasses – for CPD and post-Practitioners

- NLP In The Wild – NLP for groups in public spaces

- NLP In Practice - training days in Applied NLP

- Coaching and Therapy – one to one sessions

- Leadership Programmes – longer courses for personal and professional development, includes collective intelligence approaches and advanced NLP models and processes

- Passion in Action – social justice and change with NLP, a community leadership programme developed with Judith DeLozier

- Generative Coaching Certification – with Robert Dilts and Stephen Gilligan, sponsored in partnership with The NLP School

Courses Available

With Judith Lowe

- Coaching at Identity Level with NLP

- Conversational Belief Change with NLP

- Stress, Anxiety and Depression; Pathways to Recovery with NLP

- Cognitive Bias, Beliefs and NLP

- Theatre Skills! with NLP - for Coaches, Therapists, Speakers and Trainers

- Self-Leadership, Resilience and Vision in Challenging Times

- Effective Communication with NLP

- Enjoy Public Speaking with NLP

With the PPD Learning Training Team

- The Art of Connection with Dido Fisher

- Be More Creative; NLP Tools for Understanding Your Creativity with Jonathan Goldsmith

PASSION IN ACTION
SOCIAL CHANGE WITH NLP

With Judith Lowe and Judith DeLozier

This unique community leadership, social entrepreneurship and project development programme provides inspiration, peer support and key NLP tools - including modelling with NLP - to people who want to make a positive difference in the world.

There are three main themes:

1. Dreaming your dream - values and vision to plans and actions

2. Generative collaboration - engagement, innovation, systemic change

3. Self-leadership - well being, energy management, communication

This three-day programme has been co-developed by Judith Lowe and Judith DeLozier, who have trained it both together and individually with numerous groups over the last ten years.

Many projects have evolved from dreams into plans and plans into actions across the world including:

- Building and sustaining an orphanage in the developing world

- Creating a black and ethnic minority leadership programme

- Working with underprivileged inner city children with music in after-school clubs

- Writing a book to help children understand global warming

- Developing a national membership organisation as a Community Interest Company

- Setting up a professional therapy practice to serve a specific disadvantaged community

- Developing tools to help people experience the natural world more deeply

- Integrating young adults with learning challenges into jobs in the corporate world

- Offering drama students the tools for health and self-management

- Working one-to-one with elderly stroke survivors to rehabilitate their communication skills and joie de vivre

- Building local engagement and community with sustainable, 'green' inner city living

- Working with staff and patients in locked psychiatric wards to promote healthy practices of movement, diet and emotional well being.

Find out more: www.judithlowe.com

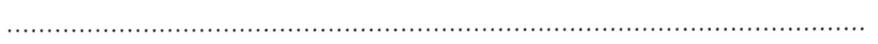

NOTES

Lightning Source UK Ltd.
Milton Keynes UK
UKHW02f1559100518

322357UK00008B/390/P